Hawaii

THE WILD PUNA COAST ON HAWAII ISLAND

HAWAII

KAUAI/OAHU/MAUI/MOLOKAI/HAWAII/LANAI

By ROBERT WENKAM

RAND McNALLY & COMPANY

Chicago · New York · San Francisco

ᵛˢ Overleaf: KANEOHE BAY, OAHU

KAMANI LEAVES, WAINIHA RIVER, KAUAI

Other books by ROBERT WENKAM

MICRONESIA: PACIFIC WILDERNESS
Photographs by Robert Wenkam,
Text by Ken Brower

MICRONESIA: THE BREADFRUIT REVOLUTION
Photographs by Robert Wenkam,
Text by Byron Baker

MAUI: THE LAST HAWAIIAN PLACE
Text and photography by Robert Wenkam

KAUAI AND THE PARK COUNTRY OF HAWAII
Text and photography by Robert Wenkam

Acknowledgment is gratefully made for permission to
reproduce historical photographs from the Baker and other
collections of the Bernice P. Bishop Museum, Honolulu, and
the Archives of the State of Hawaii; for permission from
Publishers-Hall Syndicate to quote from POGO (copyright ©,
Walt Kelly); for permission from Irving Shepard to reprint
passages from Jack London's *Stories of Hawaii*, edited by
A. Grove Day, published by Appleton-Century (copyright ©,
1965, by A. Grove Day).

Book Design by Mario Pagliai

Library of Congress Catalog Card Number: 72-4186
ISBN: 528–81989–5
Printed in the United States of America
by RAND McNALLY & COMPANY

First printing, 1972

Contents

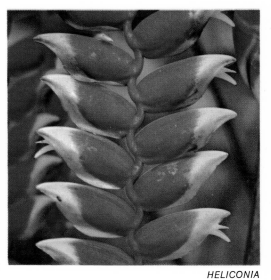

HELICONIA

My Hawaii

HIBISCUS (STATE FLOWER)

Hanalei is in some way a part of the tradition of New England. Duck ponds, weeping willows, and red Ixora still reflect the homeland of early missionaries who built their simple frame homes on Hanalei Bay. Only the tall palms speak of an easygoing island life that clashed with the Christian ethics of hard work and stern morality.

I LIVE IN HAWAII because it is the best place to live. I've visited Borneo, Hong Kong, Deadwood, South Dakota, Tahiti, and Waukegan, Illinois. Hawaii is better. If you prefer the cultural advantages of a great city, San Francisco can't be beat; but for day-to-day pleasure, with the easygoing informality of *aloha* shirts and *mu'umu'u* all year long, Hawaii is the best. Of course, there is no spring, summer, fall, or winter, and for those who like it sometimes hot, sometimes cold, this is unfortunate. The Hawaiian weather is just right all year long if you like the sun to shine most of the time. If it happens to be raining on one side of the island you can always drive over to the other side, where it probably will be dry.

It is sometimes difficult to determine in advance how much the stranger will love Hawaii. The number of visitors who have missed the return flight is unrecorded. Somehow, the love of the islands, like the love of a woman, just happens. Jack London wrote: "One cannot determine in advance to love a particular woman, nor can one so determine to love Hawaii. One sees, and one loves or does not love. With Hawaii it seems always to be love at first sight. Those for whom the islands were made, or who were made for the islands, are swept off their feet in the first moments of meeting, embrace, and are embraced."

To the visitor everything in Hawaii seems to be in the right place. The tourist from smoggy Los Angeles or Gary, Indiana, may well wonder what the local environmental fuss is all about. The ocean in Hawaii is very clear and clean (except near sugar mills). The sky is unbelievably blue all the time (except during volcanic eruptions). Nightly rain showers clean the city streets (even deadly *tsunami* waves carry away their debris), and the air smells good (especially near the pineapple cannery).

Traffic is terrible, however, and trails of black soot from jet engines seem to linger longer. Local residents cannot drive where they want to when they want to. The Honolulu traffic engineer has laced the city with one-way streets and no-left turns to such an extent that the automobile does not have the flexibility its owners pretend. Driving down Kalakaua Avenue through Waikiki is expected to be prohibited in 1973 when a pedestrian mall is constructed. Our right and freedom to do what we want is steadily being eroded. Increasing crowds of people seem to be the problem. As Pogo expressed it: "We have met the enemy and he is us." Hawaii is fast becoming the best place for too many people.

My conservationist friends will surely complain that this book isn't going to help any. Famed architect Minoru Yamasaki, a member of the National Council on the Arts, said, "Hawaii is a national treasure and must be preserved." This book will be only verifying his claim. Thousands will fly over to see for themselves. I hope they read this book first.

This book is not just another travel book. I call it a travel book with soul, because in part it is an environmental history of Hawaii. That history is a cry of pain, for the islands have been hurt. They have been trampled harshly since Captain Cook first stepped ashore almost 200 years ago. The fragile balance between native man and his environment has been seriously disturbed by the white man's use and exploitation of the islands.

No matter how we hedge our definitions—construction of hotels in front of scenic views is not an improvement on nature. Highways and airports consume irreplaceable natural scenic and recreational resources not unlike the displacement of terrain in strip mining for coal. Once the land has been disturbed, there is very little chance of restoring the landscape to its original condition. We must therefore be careful, for what we are concerned with is not only the multimillion dollar assets of a prosperous tourist industry, but our very way of life.

What the Hawaiian environmentalist is so concerned over is not so much the present—but the future. We know we've got it good. We've been to Chicago and New York and don't like what we see. We intend that Hawaii remains the best place.

Hawaii is getting crowded, but Hawaii isn't too full—yet. There is still room at the inn. But the day is not far off when there will be no more room for more inns.

Reservations are already required for visiting Hawaii (hotel rooms and airline seats). We could always add more rooms, and I'm sure Boeing will oblige with larger jets. But there is only so much space on the beach, and we don't know how to build more beaches—and that includes the Corps of Engineers, which has failed miserably in attempting to create sand. Neither have we learned how to grow one-hundred-year-old banyan trees or make surf or create the song of birds heard nowhere else on earth. When all else is lost, we do have the technological ability, such as that recommended by the Hawaii governor's marine consultant, to place ourselves in apartments on a floating island city, or for that matter, even in orbit; but these final solutions to an uninhabitable urban environment, such as dehumanizing apartment cells, must be considered for what they are—a last resort when we have exhausted the natural resources of earth and failed completely in the basic fundamentals of good housekeeping on our island.

Someday very soon the residents of Hawaii will determine an optimum residential and tourist population for Hawaii—hopefully before we are completely paved over—before the treasure is all gone. The politician's dream of an "open society" will inevitably become a nightmare without some recognition of the people-carrying capacity of the land.

While the environmentalist and the economist compare notes with the politicians, it might be prudent for the visitor to Hawaii to tread gently. These are the only Hawaiian islands we have.

R.W.

Honolulu, Hawaii

The ali'i (chiefs of Hawaii) divided the islands into pie-shaped divisions of land extending from offshore fishing grounds and lowland taro patches to the summit of central peaks. Called ahupua'a, the unique land divisions were remarkable in conception and adaptability to an island subsistence economy. The ocean surf and great kukui forests of Iao Valley are part of the great variety of resources available in a closed island ecosystem.

BISHOP STREET, DOWNTOWN HONOLULU

PARKER RANCH, WAIMEA, HAWAII ISLAND

HANALEI BEACH, KAUAI

Kauai

Garden Island

Producers of the movie South Pacific *said Kauai's north shore must surely be author James Michener's imaginary Bali Hai, where Bloody Mary welcomed American sailors. No Tahiti beach rivals Haena's unique beauty, and few islands in the fabled South Pacific can compete with the tropical image of Haena in the North Pacific.*

KAMEHAMEHA I, in legend and song the conqueror of all the islands, never conquered Kauai. Not because he didn't try. He failed in two attempts, once when his army was felled by disease and again when a rare mid-Pacific storm swamped his heavily loaded war canoes off Oahu's shore.

Then the Russians arrived. A few years after Kauai's King Kaumualii voluntarily submitted to Kamehameha's rule in 1810, an emissary of the czar built forts at the entrance to Waimea and Hanalei bays, complementing Russian occupation of Alaska and northern California.

The ruins of the Russian forts are today being reconstructed into a state park at Waimea Bay, where they serve to remind visitors of the nineteenth-century rivalry among the United States, Great Britain, France, and Russia for control of the Sandwich Islands. None of these powers gained supremacy until 1893, when American sugar barons overthrew the Hawaiian kingdom. Within seven years Hawaii became a United States territory.

Kauai still seems a little like a territory. This northernmost and oldest island in the Hawaiian chain has fortunately never been able to attract tourists on the scale of its neighbor islands. No clusters of high-rise hotels yet challenge its natural beauty, for Kauai is at the end of the airline route. Visitors are not casually stopping off on the way to somewhere else. Visitors to Kauai fly up on a spe-

cial trip because they like its unspoiled beauty. In some ways Kauai is the treasure at the end of the rainbow.

Kama'āina (Hawaii-born) residents have objected to improvement of Kauai's small airport to handle overseas jets, and they look at proposed interisland ferry operations as threats to a cherished easygoing life-style. They are frightened at what ferryloads of cars from congested Honolulu can do. They have begun to worry about the adverse side effects of population growth. Conversation about "how big should we be?" is shared with their concern for jobs.

No scarring highway pierces the incredible beauty of Kauai's north shore. Hawaiians called the cliffs *Na Pali* (the greatest cliffs), and their ruggedness has blocked man's destructive highway technology ever since the first car arrived. Only a narrow clinging trail ventures into the wilderness. Even the trail stops beyond Kalalau, where steep-walled valleys end over the sea-level beach—a hundred feet above the surf.

Hawaiians inhabited these narrow canyons a hundred years ago, raising taro prized throughout the kingdom. Today only abandoned agricultural terraces and eroded graves remain, the isolated silence shattered only by the noise of helicopters bringing in sightseeing tourists.

Covering central Kauai is Alakai Swamp, a vast mountain plateau, from which slender waterfalls thread down rock crevices. Mount Waialeale, where automatic rain gauges have recorded the highest annual rainfall on earth, dominates the summit area of the swamp, a mountaintop bog supporting indigenous dwarf *'ōhi'a-lehua* trees, fly-eating plants, and rare birds. Trout flourish in the cold streams draining into Waimea Canyon, gouged out of the red, weathered volcanic rock and cinder into a Grand Canyon of the Pacific.

Cash crops cover the flatlands in a green carpet, sometimes shaggy where sugar is dominant, etching a strong geometrical pattern at the places where pineapple grows best. Pastures soften the fields between and offer green belts for the spreading subdivisions that are tentatively reaching beyond established roads. Kauai's gentleness is not breached by clashing high-rise structures, for wise planning commissioners and county councilmen have successfully resisted pleas of developers to build higher than forty feet. The entire island is a rural garden.

Numerous private and public gardens have given Kauai a well-deserved reputation as the "garden island." Congress authorized the new Pacific Botanical Garden near Lawai, overlooking Robert Allerton's world-famed private garden. A miniature example of Allerton's vast

collection of trees and flowers from around the world can be seen in the public gardens of an old plantation mansion, the Olu Pua Gardens in the hills above Kalaheo. Front-yard gardens display the exotic seasonal variety of blooms carried to Hawaii by Kauai residents returning from world travels.

Orchids rather than geraniums are common, but the indiscriminate introduction of exotic biota has opened a botanical Pandora's box, where tiny flowering plants from temperate climates have become destructive pests in Hawaii's gentle weather. Without freezing weather and natural enemies, scrubs become trees and decorative fruits grow into impenetrable brambles smothering out and killing fragile endemic plant life.

It was the threat of hydroelectric dams in Alakai Swamp and a road around the island for tour buses that brought on the campaign to create a Kauai national park—to protect forever from economic exploitation the great mountainlands of Kauai, the swamps, the canyons, and the hidden hanging valleys of Na Pali, some so narrow that today they are still inaccessible. Their precipitous topography even stops the omnipresent tourist helicopter from intruding into their isolated meadows, little changed from the days fifty years ago when the last Hawaiian left Na Pali. But the helicopters and one-day aerial tours now fly almost everywhere, and the wilderness of Kauai no longer offers a quiet sanctuary.

The proposed parkland would extend from the broad sweep of dry, white coral sand dunes at Polihale, in the west, to wet Hanalei Bay, east of Na Pali. Between is a grand sweep of cliffs swiftly rising vertically from the ocean to escape the long northern Pacific swells smashing in a white froth against the rocky barrier.

White strands of beach disappear completely in the winter, reappearing again when summer tides scour the ocean floor. Winter waves sweep across Kalalau Beach, where later visitors bask untouched in rays of the summer sun, a proscenium for the verdant amphitheater of Kalalau Valley. Waterfalls begin in the humid mist halfway up the valley side, spouting from geological fault dikes and draining the liquid heart of Mount Waialeale into the sea.

Stewart Udall, then secretary of the interior, walked to the cleared area overlooking Kalalau Valley one cloudy afternoon and watched in awe as the cloud-filled valley emptied before his eyes and a rainbow arched across the distant *pali*. He was silent no more than a second, then exclaimed for all to hear that "Nowhere in the entire national park system is there scenic beauty like this! Give me the proclamation," he urged, "I'll sign it now."

But the timid Hawaiian congressional delegation had not even introduced a bill. The Kauai Chamber of Commerce manager at the time opposed the national park and advanced an unusual argument, claiming, "the resulting publicity would attract too many tourists."

The national park idea was temporarily defeated by an alliance of sugar planters, hunters, and rancher *kama'āina* who successfully argued against "creeping federalization," and by an unfounded claim that the old family landowners had been taking excellent care of the land. Uncle Sam was not needed, they said, and the hunters continued to hunt on the landscape where birds found nowhere else on earth are in constant danger of extinction from an adversely altered environment. Two species of birds: the Kauai creeper, or *'akialoa,* and the *nuku-pu'u* sing only in Alakai Swamp, where further introduction of alien plants will destroy their unique habitat. The long, curved bill of the honeycreeper is able to reach only into the long curved blossom of the endemic *'ohe-naupaka;* should the *'ohe-naupaka* die, the honeycreeper dies.

Some unique creatures have already departed Kauai. One of the wet caves along the Haena road beyond Hanalei was the home of a dragon. Legends relate that in the old days swimmers easily identified the dragon's pool and saved themselves from capture by bathing only in the clear-water pools, as the dragon's lair was covered with a yellow scum of scales shed off the dragon's back. Today, visitors will find no scum. The waters of the pool are perfectly clear and have been so since 1898, when the Hawaiian Republic was annexed by the United States. The dragon, a loyal one, could not endure the domination of an alien race and swam to a far Pacific island where no white man had set foot.

Kauai and all the other Hawaiian islands have been badly hurt over the years. Would the land speak of how man has trampled the landscape it would be a cry of pain, for the delicate ecological balance between man and nature has been seriously disturbed by the reckless exploitation of the islands' only natural resources—the land, the water, and the scenic beauty. The cattlemen laid bare the land, the sugar barons took out the water, and now the tourist industry seeks to exploit the beauty by building a hotel on every beach and marketing the scenic birthright of a generation unborn.

It is best that Kauai continues to remain neglected by most tourists and be overly expensive for retirement. Its optimum population has already been reached. Mountain trails and shoreside coves are uncrowded. It is still possible to be alone on the beach. Distant views of mountain and valley are unbroken by intruding high-rise concrete. There is not yet sufficient traffic to require signal lights on the main street of Lihue town. The sunsets of Haena are silhouetted along Na Pali exactly as they were when Polynesians enjoyed the end of a Hawaiian day a thousand years ago. Only a strolling surfer may interrupt the view. Perhaps it is still possible for most of the world to pass Kauai by.

Narrow, rocky, Awaawapuhi Valley is only nine airline miles from the soft, white sands of spacious Hanalei Bay on Kauai's spectacular north shore. Awaawapuhi is one of the isolated "hanging valleys" of Na Pali. It has no beach, only a broken ledge one hundred feet above the surf, where fresh mountain water drops into the perpetually wild North Pacific swells. No grazing cattle have blemished its wildness. Even thorny lantana, a pest in every other valley, is scarce in Awaawapuhi. Ancient Hawaiian agricultural terraces are the only evidence of man, for the valley is inaccessible by land or sea to all except the most adventurous. Even the noisy helicopter cannot encroach upon the privacy of Awaawapuhi—there is no flat place to land—the valley is too narrow. Hanalei Bay is the public place; a calm anchorage for pleasure boats; a sheltered cove to sail, with a wide beach two miles long —long enough to be alone on, wide enough for a busload of people. No high-rise condominiums blemish its village atmosphere; no traffic jams pollute. Hanalei is near the end of the road, where the flowers are, at the beginning of paradise.

On opposite sides of Kauai Island, ocean currents and volcanic cliffs create contrasting shorelines carved by long ocean swells spawned in the far north. At Haena, lacy ironwood (Casuarina) trees reveal the reef-protected beach where only a narrow sandspit separates ocean waves from the forested shore. On the west side the dunes at Barking Sands edge an unfriendly and dangerous surf without a protective reef. Deep waters hide undersea nuclear submarine target ranges, and supporting operations often close the dunes for public use. Strewn with strands of morning glory, the shifting dunes really do bark—footsteps in the coral-granule sands produce a distinctive "arf" on dry summer days. Beyond at Polihale, Na Pali cliffs begin.

From the high eroded plateau draining Alakai Swamp to the pandanus-shaded sands of Lumahai, Waikoko Beach is only a few miles —but the difference in elevation dramatically reveals the variety of Kauai's geography. Waimea Canyon is often described as Hawaii's Grand Canyon, and the eroded red earth and black stratified volcanic rock are a geological history of Kauai spread open by the Waimea River flowing swiftly within a half-mile-deep gorge. Waterfalls mark the upper reaches of small side canyons, some, like Waipoo Falls, visible only after heavy rains overflow the irrigation ditch piercing the north rim.

CROTON

The fern jungle of Alakai Swamp grows in a tangle of native trees atop an impervious bog that quickly collects the tremendous runoff of steady rain blown westward from Mount Waialeale. A great network of streams and rivers carries the water from numerous waterfalls that drain the high mountain swamp. The record one-year rainfall for Mount Waialeale is reported to be over 900 inches—the wettest place on earth. Rain gauges on the summit have recorded a yearly average of more than 450 inches.

WAILUA FALLS

ALAKAI SWAMP

SCAEVOLA KAUAIENSIS, ALAKAI SWAMP

Fifty years ago perhaps a thousand Hawaiians lived in Kalalau Valley, growing taro in dozens of terraced patches on the valley floor, cultivating sweet potatoes, and collecting 'opihi, crabs, and other abundant seafood from the shore. The Hawaiians lived in a self-contained community, where meandering walls of lichen-covered fieldstone protected housesites from domesticated pig and goat. All their daily needs were provided for by the land, in a gentle climate befitting the traditional rural lifestyle. In later years grazing cattle broke down the terraced walls, and the carelessly introduced exotic shrubs smothered fragile native plants, covering the valley floor with thorny thickets of lantana and guava. Only the light-green endemic kukui tree rose above the botanical debacle.

RED TI

The taro farmers and ranchers soften the natural rugged beauty of Kauai with geometric patterns of taro patches and close-cropped pastures, complementing the solid green blanket of sugarcane and orderly gray rows of pineapple covering the flatlands north and west of Lihue town. The Hanalei River provides irrigation water for the largest taro-growing area in Hawaii. Across the island at Kipu, cattle graze in the shadow of the Hoary Head range and Norfolk Pines half a century old.

Starting at the end of the paved road past Hanalei, eleven miles of trail constructed by early Hawaiian residents of Kalalau Valley span the distance between wilderness and civilization. Where Kalalau Beach sands end against the craggy Na Pali, even the ancient Hawaiians failed to build a trail. They took an outrigger canoe to reach the wild hanging valleys beyond Kalalau where wilderness begins. In Hanalei town young "counterculture" people mix with wealthy winter residents and summer tourists at Ching Young's general store, where they receive occasional checks from home to finance their break from civilization. Hanalei is a place of escape from the contemporary world discovered by hippies and monied expatriates who both hope the single main street will never be widened and the sidewalk never paved.

And over these things Koolau was king. And this was his kingdom,—a flower-throttled gorge, with beetling cliffs and crags, from which floated the blattings of wild goats. On three sides the grim walls rose, festooned in fantastic draperies of tropic vegetation and pierced by cave-entrances—the rocky lairs of Koolau's subjects. On the fourth side the earth fell away into a tremendous abyss, and, far below, could be seen the summits of lesser peaks and crags, at whose bases foamed and rumbled the Pacific surge. In fine weather a boat could land on the rocky beach that marked the entrance of Kalalau Valley, but the weather must be very fine. And a cool-headed mountaineer might climb from the beach to the head of Kalalau Valley, to this pocket among the peaks where Koolau ruled; but such a mountaineer must be very cool of head, and he must know the wild-goat trails as well.

—Jack London

Divided by basaltic lava, the twin beaches of Lumahai and Waikoko may be the most photographed in all Hawaii. In summer months, the transparent ocean attracts picnicking couples to share the soft sand and clean waters, where encircling private landowners have always welcomed the visitors and have never erected a fence. Private owners have resisted development, but public ownership is the only guarantee that tomorrow's children will play here.

Niihau Island

FIFTEEN MILES ACROSS the channel southwest of Kauai Island lies tiny Niihau, population 237. High cliffs rise vertically on the windward side where the surf breaks from the east, the land inclining gently toward the south and flattening into spreading sand dunes along the north shore.

Scalloped beaches of white sand edged with coconut palms grace the western coastline. *Kiawe* trees cover the dreary landscape, with few man-made interruptions on the featureless plain. Not a single neon sign sullies the dark night.

Niihau Island has been so long hidden from public view that exotic visions of a privately owned South Sea paradise pervade the public press. Tropical jungles and bare-breasted Hawaiian maidens still exist here in the imagination of worldly travel writers who are never allowed to visit; but the actual facts are far different. Niihau is an overgrazed cattle ranch with few amenities worthy of the smallest Midwest cattle town. It is operated at a substantial yearly loss by the wealthy owners, Kauai's autocratic Robinson family, to preserve the jobs and rural life-style of one of the last remaining Hawaiian communities. Hawaiian is the spoken language.

It's a losing struggle. Only a few cowboys are required to round up cattle on the open range. State education and public health people complain about the island's substandard schooling and health facilities. Politicians are objecting because last year only one Democratic party vote was cast on Niihau—all the remainder being Republican, despite a statewide six-to-one vote in favor of the Democrats. To Democrats, Niihau needs a political education.

Niihau was one of several grants of land offered to overseas immigrants by King Kamehameha V, who was convinced by Boston missionaries that selling land was moral and proper. Australian Francis Sinclair liked the idea of owning his own island and convinced his family of Niihau's potential as a ranch. In 1864 they paid the king $10,000 for sole ownership, and the family moved to Niihau, where they immediately found their authority as landlords challenged by native Hawaiians, who had neither understanding nor respect for private land ownership. The land had always been theirs for growing crops and hunting as they needed to feed and clothe their families. Their only obligation had been to the chiefs, who received a share of the yams and an occasional pig.

Sinclair revived a feudal rental system and refused to recognize Hawaiian ownership of land parcels that the natives had lived on for generations but which they had neglected to legalize under new laws enacted to benefit the sugar planters. Sinclair demanded one or more day's labor a month in exchange for rights to live and hunt on Niihau. Many natives refused to comply, and few had any desire to hire out as ranch hands. Fish were plentiful in the sea and taro was easily obtained from Kauai. Sweet potatoes and yams grew alongside their grass huts, and coconuts loaded the palms overhead. Working for the Sinclair family appeared to offer nothing they did not already have in abundance.

Ranching operations virtually stopped when one elderly Hawaiian couple refused to allow cowboys to graze cattle across their *kuleana* (a land parcel granted by the king) or to even set foot upon the land they claimed as their own. The disputed strip of land, a portion of an old *ahupua'a,* a pie-shaped land division reaching from the mountains to the sea, cut off all travel from one end of the island to the other. The Sinclairs were dumbfounded when proof was offered that fifty acres of "their" land on Niihau had indeed been granted to the Papapa family by King Kamehameha IV in 1855, nine years before the Sinclairs' purchase. In selling Niihau, Kamehameha V apparently had overlooked the earlier grant, and the new owners were now challenged by two hostile natives who refused to allow them even a right-of-way across the narrow parcel.

Francis Sinclair discussed his problems with Vlademar Knudsen, a white "chief" on Kauai. Sinclair was willing to pay $1,000 for the land, though the entire island had sold for only $10,000. Knudsen was held in high esteem by the Hawaiians, and his ability to negotiate was legendary. He asked Sinclair to bring him the $1,000 in silver coins.

Arriving on Niihau, Knudsen traveled overland on horseback to the Papapa's grass hut along the western shore and introduced himself. As he talked with the old couple, he carefully stacked the silver dollars in orderly rows across the *lau hala* mat spread over the floor. The old man kept shaking his head "No," emphasizing again and again his unwillingness to sell. Knudsen continued to stack the silver coins, telling the couple of the new store goods on Kauai, where the land was gentler and greener and where they could enjoy their remaining days without ever working again. The piles of coins, ten to a stack, grew on the mat. The old man repeated "No," as his wife's eyes opened wide in wonder. At last Knudsen shrugged in resignation and began unstacking the coins. Suddenly, the wife uttered an ancient Hawaiian exclamation, *"Kā!"* reached out, and pulled the treasure into her lap. The Sinclairs finally owned all of Niihau.

They soon became aware that Niihau was not a very profitable ranch and purchased the Makaweli grant across the channel on Kauai, probably the most valuable single parcel on Kauai, stretching from the Waimea River to Olokele and Hanapepe and from Waialeale summit to the sea. The Sinclairs' children married Robinsons, and today the family's lands on Kauai and Niihau total a little less than 100,000 acres, valued at many millions of dollars.

Niihau is an easy life for the Hawaiian families who choose to remain on the isolated private island ranch. Living conditions differ little from rural western towns of a hundred years ago, with whitewashed, single-wall plank plantation-style homes, sited haphazardly along dusty unpaved roads. Children walk to the single multigrade schoolhouse and fathers ride to work on a horse. The mothers stay at home to tend the garden and the house. To the social "do-gooders," Niihau is obviously a primitive island in need of civilizing.

Apparently most, if not all, Niihau residents feel fortunate at having so far escaped the blessings of civilization. None have complained and few have moved away from the island that's without telephones, private automobiles, or paved streets. No traffic lights exist on Niihau. No high-rise apartments, hotels, or police. No crime, no bars, no hippies, and no tourists. In some ways, perhaps, Niihau is a paradise, yet if measured by current American materialistic standards the island is poverty stricken. Judged by old-fashioned qualities that highly value family life and close community relationships, Niihau must be the paradise many of us are searching for but will never see. Niihau's owners allow no visitors—tourists are not welcome in paradise.

NIIHAU ISLAND

The overgrazed pastures of Honolulu in 1915 are covered by the 1972 condominium skyline.

A Fragile State

A PROPER DESCRIPTION of Hawaii is the revelation of a life-style housed on a string of semitropical islands floating in just the right place. Hawaii is not in the South Pacific—where it is too humid. It is not far into the North Pacific—where it is too cold. Nor is it in a region where stormy seas and typhoons rage. Hawaii boasts no seasons. The climate is so good native Hawaiians had no word for weather. The living is so good they had no swear words.

Missionaries put clothes on native girls over 150 years ago and invented the *holokū* and *mu'umu'u,* both long shapeless smocks that transform fat and thin into comfortable equals. Informal Hawaiians designed the *hikie'e*—a square sofa wide enough to sit on with feet off the floor and sufficiently soft enough to make love on. They pushed the family room out on the front porch and called the resulting wide-open living space a *lānai,* a word now part of the international language.

Missionaries came to Hawaii to do good, but many resigned from the church to do well, became prosperous in business, and introduced the concept of private property without explaining the consequences. The Hawaiians promptly lost everything—including their kingdom. The Americans moved in—but the Chinese were the first to commercially grow sugar; the Spaniard Don Marin planted Cayenne pineapple; and the Portuguese brought in the ukulele. No one knows who built the first travelers' lodge, but the monarchy financed the first luxury hotel in the 1870s.

It all began years ago, when Yankee sailing ships were Hawaii's transportation link with California. Honolulu Harbor was a major crossroads port of the Pacific. During the bubonic plague scare at the turn of the century, territorial health authorities identified waterfront rats as the culprits and, to clean out the rats, the Honolulu Chamber of Commerce sponsored a voluntary one-cent-a-ton tax on all cargo shipped over Honolulu docks. The cleanup campaign was successful, but the tax was not repealed, and there was soon a problem of what to do with the money. In 1920 the chamber agreed to use the surplus rat funds to establish a tourist bureau to bring in tourists.

The Matson Lines soon expanded its passenger operations and created Waikiki as a resort destination, building new Moana and Royal Hawaiian hotels for its ships to fill. Skillful advertising and promotion quickly made Hawaii a "South Pacific paradise," and exotic images of grass skirts and *hula* girls spread across the mainland.

The first small black and white advertisements appeared in *Sunset* magazine. National color spreads appeared later, created by the best photographers in the country. Anton Bruhl did most of his photography in New York. Everything Hawaiian was shipped to him—*hula* skirts, coral, coconuts, fish nets, and all the visual ingredients of a Hawaiian landscape, including the little grass shack. When Pan American airlines began operating giant flying boats across the Pacific, plumeria and ginger flowers were shipped by air daily to his East Coast studio.

Famed photographer Edward Steichen, founder of the New York Museum of Modern Art's photography department, photographed his national color advertisements in Hawaii. The subject was to become a popular classic over the years—Waikiki Beach, with an outrigger canoe and Diamond Head. Mainland editors loved it. A Steichen photo of model Jinx Falkenburg at Waikiki became a *Saturday Evening Post* cover. Hawaii became the dream vacation.

But the promoters had their problems. For one thing the old tourist bureau forbade photographers to show a dark-skinned Hawaiian beachboy on the same surfboard with a white girl. Local beachboys were always at arm's length from visitors. In later years photographers for tourist advertising were cautioned not to show Diamond Head with high-rise buildings obstructing the view. The hotels for tourists were getting in the way of the scenery they came to see.

Other problems appeared over the years. The visitor should know that tourism is the citizen conservationist's greatest challenge. Tourism has become an industry symbolic of scenic trespass, overuse, and environment exploitation. Claiming to be a "clean" industry when compared with conventional industrial activity, its traffic noise, jet exhaust fumes, "scenic" highway construction, and reckless destruction of visual beauty are seldom mentioned when adding up the financial gains to Hawaii.

Major airlines are committed to filling the seats of expensive Boeing 747 jets regardless of the adverse consequences to Hawaii's fragile and priceless scenic beauty. Absentee hotel operators maximize profits at the expense of Hawaii's easygoing island way of life, trampling the "*aloha* spirit" that once made every visitor a friend rather than the source of a large tip. The tourist industry and its tax-financed marketing agent, the Hawaii Visitors Bureau, advertise the "golden people" of Hawaii not unlike a supermarket bargain. Hotel developers carelessly mine the best beaches and scenic beauty as an inexhaustible natural resource instead of a fragile and limited asset.

The economic activity generated by Hawaii tourism exceeds an estimated $1.4 billion a year. Over 1½ million tourists visited Hawaii in 1971, leaving behind some $570 million in cash. They returned home with happy memories worth a lifetime. But a little less of Hawaii remained unspoiled.

Continued growth of Hawaii's tourist industry may be good dreaming for the land developer, but to the environmentalist it is a nightmare. An actual computer projection based on the last ten years' tourist growth rate reveals that business will be very good 100 years from today, when 60,450,000,000,000 (60 trillion, 450 billion) tourists will visit Hawaii. Nine million visitors will deplane at Honolulu International Airport every hour! The computer at the state Department of Planning and Economic Development was unable to determine what this will do to Hawaii's environment, for it cannot produce a printout of the quality of life. The programmers are unable to punch love, beauty, and the *aloha* spirit into a computer tape.

The same computer warns Oahu residents who continue buying cars at the 1970 rate that they face a bleak future in thirty years. If by the year 2001, the state Department of Transportation has succeeded in constructing sufficient highways capable of accommodating every car then on the island, all of Oahu, except for the mountaintops, will be paved over!

Perhaps the projecting is absurd. Even if it is, the reckless economic philosophy of growth *ad infinitum* must be seriously questioned—not the environmentalists' cries of alarm. If being paved over is not a desirable objective, when does the paving stop? When will the warning signs be erected to slow the growth rate to stabilize the population and to prove the computer wrong? It may already be too late for Waikiki. In fledgling resort areas around the Pacific rim, Waikiki is already a well-worn adjective describing how not to do it.

Financier Chinn Ho, president of Hawaii's Capital Investment Company, said let's accommodate the tourists! He organized the Diamond Head Improvement Association to obtain city resort zoning at the foot of Diamond Head to build high-rise hotels. Improvement—that's what the National Natural Landmark needed! The citizens said "no," in a stormy series of public hearings that culminated in the election of a new mayor who sided with the campaign to save Diamond Head. For the first time in a controversial issue, the Hawaii Visitors Bureau testified against the building of more hotels. So did the Chamber of Commerce and the building trade unions. The Save Diamond Head Association, composed of forty community groups, had acquired some unusual support in quashing the old economic philosophy that more hotels were good—no matter where.

Local militant conservationists decided the tax-supported Hawaii Visitors Bureau was

In fifteen years Kaanapali on West Maui changed from a kiawe thicket and cane field into a multimillion-dollar luxury resort. Only the beach remains untouched.

Princeville at Hanalei golf course respects the natural contours of the landscape while also providing a very scenic game.

promoting tourism and neglecting the interests of island residents, so they organized the underground Hawaii Residents' Bureau and distributed thousands of handbills on the mainland urging potential visitors to "Please don't visit Hawaii until we are able to save what's left! . . . You can't buy ALOHA!" The leaflet pictured canned "instant imitation Aloha in heavy syrup distributed by friendly skies Air Pollution Corp." There is no evidence that anyone changed his vacation plans, but the annual economic report of a Honolulu bank did remark that 1971's lower tourist growth was partly due to "derogatory comments" by conservationists.

The international environmental organization Friends of the Earth inspired legislation to collect a tourist head tax of five dollars a day, earmarked to purchase parklands and open space for public use. At the first legislative hearings only one conservationist appeared to testify. No one else. The next year the lone conservationist was joined by an AFL-CIO labor leader, organizer of the hotel and restaurant workers. He also supported the idea. The third year, advocates of the tax were heartened by attendance of Honolulu's newly elected mayor, speaking for a tax of $2.50 a day and urging that "tourism pay its own way." The tourist industry screamed, forecasting economic disaster and erosion of the "aloha spirit." The politicians obediently pigeonholed the bill for another year, noting that it did not appear to be a solution to the problem.

Of course, the problem is one of too many tourists, who provide jobs for too many residents on a group of islands too small to lodge everyone. "The loveliest fleet of islands that lies anchored in any ocean," as Mark Twain exclaimed, is in trouble.

But the mainlander, sick of crime, prejudice, and pollution in his own hometown, clamors for escape to Hawaii. The "South Pacific paradise" created by publicity flacks is still the end of the rainbow. Never mind that Hawaii's *Aloha* Week is celebrated with plastic *leis* from Hong Kong and the "fresh" *mahimahi* fish on café menus is often shipped frozen from Taiwan. So the "Hawaiian" pageantry is fake, embellished with imitation warrior helmets of dyed chicken feathers; but the rainbows and flowers and surf are real. So are the scenery and the gentle people who seem not to mind this intrusion on their island home. The soft landscape seems forever green, the rivers and streams bright and clear, where every day is a sleepy Sunday and the winter week a shirt-sleeved summer.

It is paradise for the lazy, where the poor still live in shacks and sponge on the rich, swim in nothing, and revel with a conscience comparable to a myna bird's.

Instead of concrete there are coral and sand to walk upon. There are the romantic fragrances of ginger, *pīkake,* and plumeria mingling with fresh trade winds blowing over snowy summits and through rustling woodlands spared from volcanic wrath. Who can resist paradise?

Mark Twain said of the visitor to Hawaii, ". . . when you are in that blessed retreat, you are safe from the turmoil of life; you drowse your days away in a long deep dream of peace; the past is a forgotten thing, the present is heaven, the future you can leave to take care of itself. You are in the center of the Pacific Ocean; you are miles from the world; as far as you can see, on any hand, the crested billows wall the horizon, and beyond this barrier the wide universe is but a foreign land to you, and barren of interest."

An English captain, James Cook, discovered Hawaii for the Western world. The Polynesians discovered it for themselves much earlier and ended their Pacific migration. There was no better place to go. Now an overpopulated America has rediscovered Hawaii's delicious living-style and wants to share the dessert.

Conceding as we do that we are the world's most intelligent creatures, we should be bright enough to give this reverence for life and nature a better try. Dave Brower, founder

of Friends of the Earth, says, "Perhaps it is about time for man to try to come back to his senses, all of them. Better that he does, before becoming too enamoured of his overriding technology and overbearing intellect.

"What we need is not an expanding economy, but an expanding individual," cautions Brower. "The individual can expand and have no trouble understanding other living things, if he can manage to renounce some of his dependence on man-made ephemera and to spend more time with things as they were, are, and may still be."

It is not too late to leave Hawaii alone. Not too late to refuse domination by an insane economy of growth and technological madness which discards every quality that is wholesome, beautiful, and good, in the name of profit and progress. There must not be a hotel on every beach—or a road on every mountain. To allow every visitor equal access to Hawaii is to destroy Hawaii. To allow in every visitor who has a ticket will destroy a national treasure. At some point in time—maybe not this year—but perhaps soon—the people of Hawaii must say, "No! There is no more room at the inn."

Mokuaikaua Church, oldest in the islands, is still a landmark more than 150 years after being built on Kailua, Kona's main street.

YESTERDAY'S PIONEER HOTEL

WAIKIKI BEACH, OAHU, ABOUT 1900

The Gathering Place

COCONUT

The surf at Waikiki is the same water as the water anywhere in Hawaii, but at Waikiki the water and the surf seem particularly delightful—it is wonderful water. It is cool enough for a long swim and warm enough for a quick dip without hesitation. Night or day it is always the same temperature—just right.

THE BEST WAY to fly to Honolulu is take the jet to Hilo on the island of Hawaii. Western Airlines leaves San Francisco at 2:15 in the afternoon, arriving in Hilo just before sunset. A short flight northwest toward Honolulu at twilight, flying high over every island except Kauai, is an unusual scenic offering at no extra fare; an ideal perch to absorb a little of what this group of islands floating in the Pacific is all about. The islands are all in place, arranged as the Polynesian demigod Maui left them after a fishing trip, with the largest and highest volcanic island carefully located over a hot spot on the ocean floor.

Honolulu is an ocean-oriented city as far away as you can get—no city is farther from a continent. It is an old seaport town in the mid-Pacific, grown to maturity. It is a big city, but it retains many of the pleasant attributes of a small town while offering cultural amenities and entertainment comparable to cities with much larger populations.

Honolulu is a beautiful city, physically and socially. There are no slums or racial ghettos. It is clean, swept by trade-wind showers when the city forgets. Strung for twenty-two miles along an undulating leeward shore between perpetually blue ocean and ever-green hills, the city is comparable to a grand stage, with backdrops of fluted cliffs and deep valleys. A curtain of fluffy clouds drops over the mountains at night to loosen cooling showers drifting seaward over a sleeping city. Rainbows are made at sunset. Liquid sunshine is the rain falling at Waikiki.

The Hawaiian's ethnic influence is evident everywhere. All place-names are Hawaiian. By city ordinance subdividers must use Hawaiian street names, posing an increasingly difficult problem because the Hawaiian language provides only 26,000 words, many impossibly long for the standard street sign. North and south are unknown, although Hawaii's segment of the interstate freeway has introduced east and west. Toward the ocean is *makai;* toward the mountains is *mauka.* South is Diamond Head, and the opposite direction refers to *Ewa* sugar fields beyond Pearl Harbor.

Easy walking trails penetrate the mountain forest on every ridge. Within minutes the casual stroller can escape Waikiki traffic noise and crowded apartments to experience the soft quiet of tropical woods releasing mixed fragrances of wild fruit and flowering ginger. History is very close. Notched ridges still provide holding caches for the sling rocks of Hawaiian warriors. Pearl Harbor reflects the distant *Arizona* memorial, identifying a place of a more recent war and the tomb of over a thousand sailors. It is only the turn of a head to wild thimbleberries growing profusely in thickets under a tropical canopy. Hard-shelled *kukui* nuts cover the earth beneath indigenous candlenut trees utilized a hundred different ways by the Hawaiians. Scratchy staghorn fern shakes off the remnants of early morning showers in the shimmering wet forest where Oahu's wild beauty is revealed most delightfully to the hiker who allows musty smelling overripe guava to squish upward between his bare toes.

Honolulu's maverick mayor, Frank Fasi, an Italian ex-marine married to probably the most beautiful Japanese girl in Hawaii, is not one to dodge controversial decisions or bow to sacred institutions. He moved, despite objections, the Kodak *hula* shows out of the public park where they had promoted film sales for twenty years. He tore down Waikiki's decrepit Queen's Surf nightclub, revered by thousands of servicemen and habitués of the "barefoot bar." He told the state to stop work on the cross-island interstate freeway because the county General Plan was ignored. He stopped the seemingly irresistible march of concrete condominium walls around Diamond Head by calling for the expansion of Kapiolani Park to include all the elite residential lots along the Diamond Head shore beyond Waikiki Beach. Many lots are still to be purchased by the city in the estimated $15-million park expansion, but already almost a mile of Kalakaua Avenue, the main street of Waikiki, opens directly upon the beach without any obstructing buildings—twice the open space of twenty years ago.

Waikiki itself is physically and socially almost an island city. Mostly a reclaimed swamp and duck pond, it is a self-contained flamboyant resort, in contrast to the staid financial and political atmosphere of downtown Honolulu four miles to the north. Ala Moana shopping center, one of the world's largest, spans the space between the two cities with a multilayer splurge of shops that boggles the imagination. It is almost a third city, attracting customers from every district of Honolulu and dramatically revealing the amazing racial mix of Hawaii.

Across the island through twin highway tunnels piercing the Koolau mountains are Kailua and Kaneohe, bedroom suburbs rapidly sprawling northward across the flatlands between the mountains and the sea. The two communities justify to highway planners searching for federal tax monies the need for a ridiculous extension of the expensive interstate highway system. Beginning in Honolulu, the nine miles of proposed six freeway lanes would end abruptly at Kaneohe Bay. An ocean gap of 2,400 nautical miles remains to be bridged to reach Seattle's unfinished I-90 stub, on the shore of Lake Washington. I-90 begins in Boston.

Honolulu, Hawaii's capital, may be the "longest" city in the world. It includes the Hawaiian Islands National Wildlife Refuge and extends about 1,400 miles to Kure Island, northwest of Midway. The city and county of Honolulu includes all of the island of Oahu, where 82 percent of Hawaii's population lives, mostly in a densely congested area along the southwest shore.

When Honolulu councilmen and state legislators meet across the street from each other in the spring, it is quite evident that political duplication is expensive. Overlapping governmental services have been mostly eliminated, but the two highway departments continue to confuse jurisdictions. Honolulu (the city) has a rapid transit rail system in design that Hawaii (the state) feels is unnecessary. The mayor wants a halt to freeway building, while the governor seems willing to pave the island over to accommodate private cars. A bill was introduced in a recent state legislative session to abolish all counties and in effect end the debate about who takes care of things. It died in committee.

The unspoiled green hills—many free of housing—rising majestically behind Honolulu, are no accident. They were saved from proliferating subdivisions by the outcry of aroused citizens and the fortunate appointment of a state Land Use Commission that included a militant, independent conservationist. One environmental vote on the commission was sufficient to change the customarily urban-oriented

zoning body into a group seriously concerned with the unique natural visual resources of Honolulu. When scenic values were identified as valuable assets of the multimillion-dollar tourist investment at Waikiki, it was easy to convince the bankers and brokers that every tree and green hillside was a part of their security portfolio.

Hillsides steeper than a 20-percent slope, plus all land not in urban or agricultural use, were zoned "conservation" and placed out of immediate reach of subdividers. The landowners complained about their land being saved merely for photographs by tourists' Instamatics and used without compensation as a scenic background for Waikiki hotels; but Hawaii's state constitution clearly granted the state a legal right to "conserve and develop its natural beauty" and provided that, in the long-term best interests of the people, "private property shall be subject to reasonable regulation."

It is easy to see where conservationists lost the vote. Sprawling housing tracts intrude upon central Oahu cane lands. Paved roads wriggle up narrow ridges, never succeeding in conquering erratic volcanic topography. Tourist bird parks and research-oriented sea-life parks intrude upon the edge of wilderness. A telescope is mounted on Hawaii's highest peak, and the Air National Guard recklessly constructs obsolete radar facilities on the rim of Kauai's beautiful Kalalau Valley to intercept enemy bomber planes in a missile age. NASA operates Apollo communications facilities atop the highest point in Kokee State Park—presumably to be closer to the moon.

The famed view from Nuuanu Pali, on the cross-island road to Kailua, was saved by vote of the state Land Use Commission. City permits had been filed, subdivision lots already platted, streets named, and commercial sites selected. The banana growers and owners of picturesque dairy farms were given eviction notices. All commissioners did not agree during debate that open space at the foot of the *pali* (cliff) was of greater value than another subdivision, and the first vote on urban zoning for the *pali* view lands was split, so bargaining began in earnest. What did the development-oriented commissioners of the neighboring islands want? The deal was made. Today, somewhere on Maui, several speculative subdivisions flourish along the Kihei shore, traded for a unanimous vote to save Oahu's Nuuanu Pali view. It was a good bargain in the American tradition.

Success cannot be easily seen, for the stopped subdivision does not exist to complain about. Halted condominiums never interrupt a distant horizon line. Success in land conservation is open space, vast panoramic vistas, scenic beauty, and green valleys—the natural beauty that is taken for granted as an inherent right.

A drive over central Oahu, passing through the carefully tended sugar and pineapple plantations, offers agricultural open space and untouched mountain ridges to the west and east. The Koolaus outline the jagged lower edge of a smogless sky, hopefully perpetually blue, softened with scattered cumulus clouds where an invisible temperature change occurs overhead. In the later afternoon, rainbows commonly curve outward from the narrow western valleys, reflecting the sun retiring below the opposite Waianae rim. Beyond Wahiawa's lofty plateau can be seen the north shore. Suddenly the world is an island and the limits from shore to shore are undeniable. Oahu is finite, and the close alliance of land, sea, and people is a new discovery. The island is life, and the security of a good life is surely revealed in the excitement of going over the hill to the other side of the island.

The University of Hawaii campus seems isolated from the surrounding residential community in the same way that Waikiki is a resort city separate from Honolulu. The dense cluster of hotels along Waikiki Beach houses vacationing tourists savoring the excitement of a famous resort, while a more serious group of island visitors at the federally funded East-West Center gather to study. Foreign students from around the world live with Americans in a liberal island environment on the informal Manoa Valley campus.

Overleaf: WAIKIKI BEACH ॐ

Hawaii holds a unique status among the fifty states—Hawaii was a kingdom. Iolani Palace and throne room remain to remind visitors today of Hawaiian kings and Hawaiian queens. The heroic statue of Kamehameha I, who defeated rival ruling chiefs and created the Hawaiian kingdom, is a routine camera stop for visitors. But for Hawaiian people the monument fronting the Judiciary Building is a proud and symbolic reminder of royal heritage and is today the focal point of Hawaiian celebrations.

Flower leis and ti-leaf skirted hula dancers may be the essence of tourist Hawaii. While most nightclub "Hawaiian" hulas are imported Tahitian dances, and airport lei sellers see no ethical compromise in spraying flowers their own choice of colors from aerosol cans, the tourist is seldom aware of any deception. He enjoys the show and applauds for encores, to experience in actuality the folklore of yesterday, when the hula was a sacred art, a celebration of love. It is still an expression of personal enjoyment, learned at an early age and best danced bashfully at local family birthday luaus, when every gesture and twist sends a private message— a language for lovers. Hands tell the story: waving sea and swaying palms; a full moon and fragrant flowers; unrequited love and rendezvous with a little brown gal.

Upon the contrasting variety of island scenery and history flows an exotic blend of Asiatic flavors, mixing Oriental cultures from China, Japan, Korea, and the Philippines. The Japanese influence is dominant—they were the second group of Oriental immigrants—and today are the largest national group in Hawaii, where everyone is a minority. The cultural mix is complete when a Shinto priest enjoys the same status as a Christian, where modern apartments crowd classic pagoda shrines, and when Buddhists celebrate Christmas.

BANZAI PIPELINE, SUNSET BEACH

QUEEN'S SURF, WAIKIKI

Honolulu lives in the style of a small town, with the flourish of a famous resort and all the problems of a big city. It mixes well. It is fun. Most commuters are only a few minutes' ride from work or Waikiki, thereby transforming day-to-day living into a year around choice between the office or the beach. Tourist demands have created an exciting night life and an opportunity for Hawaiian music and dance to thrive. Local residents complain about crowds and traffic generated by tourist activity, but are quick to enjoy its benefits, like the popular Canlis restaurant in Waikiki—a favorite place for mixing with tourists.

WAIKIKI—ALA MOANA SKYLINE

Attack carrier U.S.S. Kitty Hawk *salutes the World War II Arizona Memorial in Pearl Harbor. The sunken battleship* Arizona, *its rusted hulk lying beneath the shrine and still holding its entombed crew, has never been decommissioned—her flag still flies.*

MILITARY GUARD, ARIZONA MEMORIAL

MAKAPUU BEACH, SEA LIFE PARK

KIAWE, MAKAHA VALLEY

BANANA BLOSSOM

KANEOHE BAY

65 THE GATHERING PLACE

HAWAIIAN WOMAN

HULA DANCERS

Must We Countenance the Hula?

Reprinted from
Thrum's *HAWAIIAN ANNUAL*
1918

DURING THE PAST SUMMER THE *Advertiser,* in dealing with an entertainment of varied Hawaiian attractions given in the city, took occasion to commend effort of like character embodying tableaux, oils, music and songs and innocent dances, in marked contrast to the disgusting obscene hula productions that are too often paraded before the public, and for some unaccountable reason is being introduced abroad as a society attraction. The present writer was quoted as commending the attempt to furnish such Hawaiian entertainments illustrative of ancient customs and recreations, and instanced the first effort on these very lines but a few years ago at the Young Hotel, an invitational affair by Mr. E. L. Parker, a visitor from Buffalo, as a recognition of social courtesies from Honolulu's "four hundred".

I was further quoted as 'grieved' at the apparent growing acceptance of the questionable hula, notwithstanding the protests that have been made and laws on the statute books regarding them; a result, doubtless, of the attempt to have it considered a religious ceremonial performance of the early Hawaiians, hence, by inference, innocent, a view that meets with but ridicule from those best qualified to know—the Hawaiians themselves.

With all moral questions there are always those who would obstruct the effort, and charge the would-be reformers with narrowness; interference with one's liberty, and other resentful epithets. Such was the experience attending the incident above referred to, and amid expressions of approval came a very mandatory order over the phone to "mind your own business". Evidently someone's toes had been trodden on, and a probable source of revenue, or side attraction to legitimate business, interfered with.

It comes within the province of the *Annual* to disseminate reliable information pertaining to Hawaii, and anything that is defamatory and seeks to mislead the public, makes it our business to decry such attempts, and the effort to exploit the lascivious, disgusting hula as an innocent amusement of the Hawaiian people of olden time, demands our protest in unmistakable terms, more especially as claim is made that it was "an institution of divine, that is, religious origin," and that its halls (halaus) were ever provided with an "altar as the visible temporary abode of the deity," hence, forsooth, having the approval of the gods it should by right therefore have the approval of mortals. Those who use this pretext in the endeavor to overcome the scruples of the better element, and foist the shameless thing at public gatherings as an ancient "religious" ceremony and expect unsuspecting visitors and innocent youth of both sexes to look unblush-

ingly upon it, studiously avoid the admission by the author of the above "divine" conception of the hula, that "in modern times it has wandered so far and fallen so low that foreign and critical esteem has come to associate it with the riotous and passionate ebulitions of Polynesian kings and the amorous posturings of their voluptuaries."

This in itself condemns it as an unfit exhibition for any respectable public or semi-public gathering or society function, yet under the plea of rendering an attraction for the tourist, to meet the desire of a certain class, the attempt is made to popularize it, and in doing so commercialize it in vaudeville shows and low channels, as was done last year, renders it quite time to protest, not only against the various disgusting hulas, for decency sake, but the effort to palm them off as a religious affair.

That Laka was the patron deity of the hula devotees, and its master of ceremonies a kahuna (priest), rendered it no more a religious performance than that of the canoe-building priest, which, like all Hawaiian callings also had each their special deities and invocations. Any impression therefore of the hula having any approach to a religious observance is erroneous. There was a temple service called *hulahula,* which may inadvertently have been the ground for the claim of religious character given the hula, whether of ancient or modern rendition. If such was the case, its ritual has been grossly misinterpreted, as may be seen by the following descriptive account:

"Hulahula was the name of the services of the kapu loulu, which was an important religious ceremony on questions of war or other national moment, observed in large temples like Leahi, Mookini, Puukohola and others of similar character, and in which only the high chiefs participated. The ceremony was held only at night at a time when the people were in slumber; in the solitude of night. At that time the high priest and chiefs entered the temple where the services were to be held on occasions whereby the king might learn clearly the favorable, or ill omens of coming events.

"The observance of the ceremony was so solemn and sacred that death would be meted out to the person who casually passed by; roving or disturbing animals also would be slain.

"In the evening the king made his entry into the temple. At the proper time for the service the high priest performed his duties according to the rituals of his order. If the ordinances were duly observed without interruption of any noise, the high priest would then proclaim the ceremonies perfect, auguring victory for the king in the coming battle, or other question before him."

Anyone can see at once that this religious temple service has no connection whatever with the amusement hula performances in open air, or halau, designed by the performers, with their indelicate bodily contortions to appeal to the baser passions. It is hoped therefore that no further attempt will be made to overcome public scruples of morality by any such flimsy statement of its religious origin.

There are laws on the statute books planned to license and control hula performances, but for some reason or pretext with shameless effrontery they obtrude their presence in public, and have been made the center of attraction in Carnival and Kamehameha day pageants and on other occasions.

The exhibitions of the hula at the opening night of the last Carnival drew forth the following:

"Concerning the hula dancing that was exhibited in the Palace grounds I would say no more than that I would have expected to see it somewhere in New York or Paris at ten cents or five centimes a ticket, but I was sorry to see it in Hawaii. It was about as typically a Hawaiian dance as Magna Charta was a 'scrap of paper.' Why should Honolulu show the hula in a form that we roast when we see it while traveling on the mainland?" (Extract from *Bystander,* Sunday Advertiser, Feb. 25, 1917.)

Also the following excerpts from Kahuna Nui, in the same issue:

"Mister Edditter! Here's sum thing what me and planty more Hawaiian, and kamaaina haole kicking about, and thas that HULA they having at the king palace one nite. And I think so even Kalakaua and the Kamehameha statchu get a shame on they face if they see that. It makes us Hawaiian mad and shame, but I tell you true, you haole is the fault for allowed that kine of hula jus becos it putting sum munny in you pocket. One days you tell becos the hula is bad, then nother days you get sum Hawaiian to dancing it. If hula is bad one days, then its bad for erry other days in the ears. Since the time I bin born and lived and died in Hawaii nei I never see this kine of hula what make the Hawaiian blushes underneath of they olive-brown skin."

The next day appeared this protest, signed A Hawaiian: "Editor Advertiser—I wish to second the remarks of 'Kahuna nui' in yesterday's Advertiser, in regard to the public hula exhibition given in the Capitol grounds last week as a sample of Hawaiian dancing.

"It was lewd, suggestive and disgraceful. There were no ones more disgusted with it than the Hawaiians present. They felt keenly that they were being defamed in the eyes of the visiting strangrs. It is to be hoped that future Carnival managers will see it that nothing of this kind is permitted to occur again."

Disapproval has been freely expressed, and protests from time to time appear in the daily press, as is shown, but with doubtful result. Shortly following the published account mentioned in the opening of this paper, the following note came to hand, which speaks for itself:

"It has been a great pleasure to note the recent hard knocks against the present-day hula. When occasion offered I have done my own little "bit" against the hula, insisting that no worse sort of promotion could be invented, as it panders to the worst element, not to the solid, well-behaved class that every country needs. My voice however does not go for much, the subject needed the strong voice of substantial citizens, who command respect, having great influence.

> Gratefully yours,
> Joseph Dutton."

In support of the foregoing comes an echo from abroad. Evidently there has been "a chiel among us, takin' notes," and he has printed them to our disgrace and shame, as follows, for which we are indebted to the *Star-Bulletin:*

"A vigorous campaign to stamp out the time-honored hulahula national dance of Hawaii, which is accomplished without the dancer moving his or her feet, has been instituted by clergymen and the reform element, according to Rev. Ezra Crandall, of Worcester, Mass., who arrived in San Francisco recently, after a visit of several weeks in the island capital, says the San Francisco Bulletin.

"The 'disgusting hula' of the present day, according to Rev. Crandall, is a survival of an ancient pagan ceremony practised by the Hawaiians, but it has so degenerated that it has become a moral menace. Rev. Crandall stated that it is the opinion of those conducting the campaign that every self-respecting Hawaiian should take a stand against the terpsichorean indecency involved in the native dance.

"The hula, as it is commonly danced and commonly known now," said Rev. Crandall, "should be the subject of vigorous condemnation, and I do feel that every Hawaiian should feel this reflection on the decency and propriety of his race.

"For the honor and the good name of the Hawaiian race, all men and women of Hawaiian blood are being urged to join in discountenancing these indecent exhibitions. The mere fact that some people, principally tourists, want to see them is no excuse for their existence. They are a shame to the islands."

HAWAIIAN WOMEN

HULA GIRL

A Racial Consensus

HAWAII IS WRONGLY CALLED a racial melting pot. The islands are a complex racial mix, an "island state where everyone is a racial minority," and with all minorities living together in harmonious relationships that are surely an example for the nation. The people of the Hawaiian Islands are proud of their differences, yet they all call themselves Hawaiians.

It has not always been so. For only a few years has Hawaii enjoyed its present excellent racial harmony. Almost every example of racial prejudice still existed in 1945, including poll taxes, segregated schools, and exclusive residential tracts for every race. The change came about swiftly, but gently, with none of the violence associated with contemporary mainland events.

In 1946 Honolulu department stores hired no Oriental clerks. The white-owned banks trained few Oriental employees for any position serving the public. Exceptions were obviously token. Orientals working side by side with whites were always paid a lower wage. Hawaii's largest department stores kept Orientals in the back rooms as stock clerks or bookkeepers, seldom appointing them to higher positions. Oriental brides never appeared on newspaper society pages. The best restaurants were slow to find a satisfactory table for Orientals. The prestigious Pacific and Outrigger Canoe Club banned nonwhite members altogether; the local Elks Club still bans nonwhites—and flies the Stars and Stripes from a lighted flagpole every night to protest its innocence.

As recently as 1950 one midtown department store fired its blonde saleswoman upon discovering her husband was Japanese. In the postwar years mixed racial couples sometimes found housing impossible to find. Famed author James Michener angrily left Hawaii when his request to buy a home in the wealthy, then white-only, Kahala section of Honolulu was denied. His wife was Japanese. Bishop Estate leasing agents required both husband and wife to appear in person when negotiating for homesites. If either applicant were nonwhite the lots were conveniently sold out.

Hawaii's social revolution probably began on the morning Pearl Harbor was bombed. Federal wage and price controls that were enforced during the war years suddenly ended traditional plantation life, contract labor, and economic racism. Victory in the Pacific marked the beginning of an economic and social middle class that did not exist in prewar Hawaii, as well as a two-party system, organized labor, and the tourist boom. Hawaii never returned to the "good old days" of a sugar aristocracy and the "Big Five" corporate monopoly.

Harry Bridges' International Longshoremen's and Warehousemen's Union challenged the plantations in every aspect of labor relations. Mainlanders with a billion dollars to invest in the territory joined local entrepreneurs in the creation of small businesses on every island, while white liberals opposed the racist hiring practices, the poll tax, and the "English standard" schools that segregated Orientals from whites. Union organizing committees changed overnight the discriminatory company rules that had been in force since the overthrow of the Hawaiian kingdom. The ILWU was the first to organize all races and trades into one large union. The separate racial plantation camps established by the sugar companies no longer served as the decisive instruments used to break every strike. For the first time it was "one for all, all for one."

Hawaii's Japanese veterans returned home covered with medals and citations—their units the most decorated in the war. Some came back with pretty German and Italian "war brides." Hundreds earned degrees as doctors, engineers, and lawyers at mainland universities. Politically aroused Japanese approached the dominant Republican party, where the action was. The Old-Guard Republicans replied negatively, implying they had no room in the party for Orientals. It was a rude shock for the young people of Hawaii and gave them a quick education in Establishment politics. The Republican party in Hawaii thus began its long downhill slide to virtual oblivion, but it was not until 1953 that the new Democrats achieved a legislative majority. In 1960 they defeated the Republican governor, and by 1966 all mayors were Democrats.

The young Japanese war heroes organized a progressive Democratic party with the avowed intent of securing racial equality and political power. Unlike the racially white Republican party, with token Oriental candidates only emphasizing the fact, the new Democrats accepted everyone.

In the months following the sneak Pearl Harbor attack, John Burns, an Army Intelligence officer, had convinced authorities that Hawaii's Japanese were loyal to America and halted plans to deport Japanese to mainland concentration camps. The racial prejudice exposed on the mainland's West Coast was not duplicated in Hawaii. Burns at this writing is in his second term as governor of Hawaii and receiving a substantial number of votes in every election from young Japanese-Americans grateful for his trust in their parents' loyalty.

The Hawaiian electorate votes overwhelmingly Democratic and a shade left of center. All except one of Hawaii's congressional delegation are Democrats. It speaks again of the strange contradictory qualities of Hawaii: that the only remaining important Hawaiian Republican in elective office is a Chinese—the only Chinese in Congress, Sen. Hiram Fong. He is a right-wing politician who was elected by a liberal electorate. Fong campaigned as a "local boy" who made good. His mainland-born opponent didn't stand a chance.

• • •

Governor John Burns runs what he calls a "consensus" administration—a winning formula. With streamlined state departments and a small cabinet, without the political opportunism generated by far-flung townships and autonomous counties, the voters' influence in governmental activities is felt to a far greater degree than in the states of the mainland. The consensus philosophy of government has resulted in some strange compromises and bitter controversies, but at the same time the newly emerging middle class has achieved success and prosperity in a booming economy.

The New England town-hall style of government, with direct participation by active citizens, is fast disappearing in America's increasingly complex society. It thrives in Hawaii. Hawaii has simplified the government of people. It is relatively easy for the public to reach the political leadership and difficult for the bureaucrat to push his responsibilities aside to another agency or political subdivision. Civil servants cannot blame the city for a state problem when no city exists—there are no incorporated cities or towns in Hawaii. The county cannot be criticized for basic zoning regulations—land zoning is a state responsibility. The old political shell game of "passing the buck" stops early in Hawaii—elected officials must face the wrath of voters at the polls for specific acts of malfeasance.

Some problems of political jurisdiction do exist in Hawaii. When southerly winds pile high the beaches with seaweed, the smell will sometimes remain for days while county and state officials debate who shall clean the beaches. The question has been unresolved for years. No one has yet decided who will administer the largest park in downtown Honolulu—Ala Moana Park is still half state and half county park. The inefficient practice of county road crews mowing grass on road shoulders and state employees cutting grass on highway bridge approaches was solved only recently by assigning county work crews to cut all the grass with state-owned mowers. On many islands county workers drive state trucks.

There are no state police or sheriffs—only county police. Nor separate school systems or county hospitals, nor special tax assessments to support schools or public facilities. All monies come out of the general fund in lump-sum appropriations. There is no sales tax—

only a 4 percent gross business excise tax that almost everyone passes on.

All taxes are collected by the state, except for automobile license and business fees paid directly to the counties. County governments set property-tax rates, but the state collects the taxes and remits to the counties all the cash plus whatever additional funds the state legislature deems appropriate to meet county expenses and capital improvements.

All land in the state, both public and private, is zoned by the state. The state Land Use Commission, appointed by the governor and confirmed by the state senate, determines urban boundaries of all cities and towns and zones all agricultural and "conservation" lands. (It has classified perhaps 50 percent of the islands as conservation land to protect scenic resources, open space, and flood plains.) No "conservation" zoned land can be used without permission. Under penalty of law no chain saw can fell a tree. The over-permissive administrator finds his every act covered by four TV stations, nineteen radio stations, and two daily English newspapers that together constitute the most environmentally concerned media in the country.

The Chamber of Commerce joined community groups in helping to enact one of the most restrictive business sign ordinances anywhere. The Chamber then joined with the Sierra Club and other conservation organiza-

HAWAIIAN

tions in supporting statewide zoning and the halting of high-rise condominium construction around the base of Diamond Head. Maybe it can be said that in some ways Hawaii is also a "consensus" community.

It doesn't all work perfectly. The Chamber of Commerce and the citizen environmental organizations still have to publicly criticize the mayor and governor for unwarranted concessions to landowners and real estate speculators.

Hawaii invented condominiums; was the first state with a long-range general plan for land use; was the first to abolish archaic abortion laws; was the first to enact statewide zoning. Billboards have been outlawed in Hawaii for over forty years, and the only political campaign posters permitted in Honolulu are bumper stickers. An aerial advertising firm was boycotted out of existence in two weeks. The "fast-buck" speculative subdivider sells his lots warily in the islands, knowing that many of his fellows have suffered considerable loss when challenged by alert government officials and citizen conservationists. The "fast-buck" comes with difficulty.

• • •

The countryside blooms with the fragrance of myriad alien flowers imported by the original immigrant contract sugar workers and recent travelers from everywhere. Residents have created by accident an exotic botanical treasure that complements the blend of Europeans and Asians and Polynesians in a neo-Hawaiian race.

In still primitive islands of the Micronesian Pacific, misplaced Western ideals have begun to destroy remote island communities, for the natives are doubting the worth of their own culture in the quest for Western clothing, Western language, and imported products that demand a money economy.

Hawaii in the same era has evolved a contemporary life-style, in which its residents enjoy perhaps the highest per capita income in the nation. The highest paid agricultural workers in the world grow and harvest Hawaii's sugarcane and pineapple. An elegant mix of cultures and races from every continent, all in the flux of a prosperous economy, has blended philosophical and social values of the East and the West. Judeo-Christian materialism, mingled with Buddhism and Oriental mysticism, in a Western mold of ethics, is giving new meaning to traditional concepts of constitutional rights and privileges.

Interracial harmony has not extinguished the racial differences. It is these very differences that make Hawaii an exciting place to live. Integration is a meaningless term in Honolulu where Japanese, Chinese, Filipino chambers of commerce operate. It is the

elaborate yearly ethnic festivals, financed in part by legislative appropriated tax monies, that help perpetuate the unique racial differences. Hawaii celebrates the Japanese Cherry Blossom Festival and Chinese New Year as community events. The Buddhists use Kapiolani public park to commemorate the enlightenment of Siddhartha Guatama, the Buddha. The Samoans have their own Flag Raising Day. The Fiesta Filipina is a month-long Filipino celebration following Lei Day, when the unique Hawaiian contribution of *aloha* is demonstrated with flower garlands of every imaginable combination. The mainland *haole,* as whites are called in Hawaii, have Halloween and St. Patrick's Day. Everyone celebrates Christmas. But the Hawaiians have little to celebrate during the elaborate pageantry of Prince Kuhio and Kamehameha days when they resurrect memories of past royalty.

• • •

Native Hawaiians have arrived at the bottom of the economic ladder. The once proud Polynesian people, whose ancestors sailed thousands of miles across the ocean to establish a Hawaiian kingdom, are all too often today seen on their hands and knees scrubbing the floor of a resort hotel suite. The names of applicants for low-cost government housing are mostly Hawaiian. The police blotter is spotted with Hawaiian surnames. Too many Hawaiians drop out of school—few are in the professions. Reverend Akaka, State Senator Poepoe, Father Kekumano, and contractor Akiona are among the few exceptions. The politicians pay token obeisance to the Hawaiian "vote," but it is so fragmented that its influence is barely noticed at the polls.

The Hawaiians lost a kingdom to American colonists without firing a shot. There was little opposition. Immigrant sugar workers precipitated considerable organized violence in response to repressive labor conditions on the sugar plantations. The Hawaiians simply walked off the fields and went fishing. The sugar barons took their land. The Hawaiians grumbled and disappeared into city ghettos. The Hawaiian Homestead Act was passed to give them an opportunity to return to the land. Few did. Many immediately subleased their acreage to large corporate pineapple growers. Large parcels were made available for industrial use by other races. Most homestead lands still remain unoccupied, while hundreds of Hawaiian families live in crowded and substandard city dwellings.

Hawaiians as a group first began to display signs of resentment in recent years, when the state legislature, concerned over the rising cost of land and scarcity of fee simple residential lots, introduced measures to break up the tremendous Bishop Estate—the trust for

consider mainlanders somewhat of a curiosity anyway, so a mutual feeling of open expression, in Hawaii, becomes "aloha."

Four long-haired mainland "hippies" have been shot and killed in Hawaii, so the traditional welcome isn't quite extended by everyone to everyone; but the unrestrained greeting to strangers is so widespread that an "aloha spirit" indigenous to the islands undoubtedly does exist beyond tourist-industry platitudes.

It is not unusual for residents to drive clear across the island to show their favorite waterfall to a chance acquaintance. Many tourists return home with stories of favors done and services volunteered that appear inspired only by the joy of doing. It does add luster to the "golden people."

The people of Hawaii are proud of their home and proud of their race and country. Pride and racial integrity create confidence and self-esteem. Sharing the wealth and beauty of Hawaii, even with strangers, becomes second nature. After all, Hawaii is the only state that has the historical and cultural heritage of an independent kingdom to offer.

20 percent of privately held lands, Princess Bernice Pauahi Bishop's inheritance. Kamehameha Schools, the estate's only beneficiaries, are among the few schools in America today where admission is based on race. Applicants must be at least part Hawaiian. The schools' instructors must be Protestants, in keeping with the will of the Hawaiian princess.

The law to permit leaseholders to buy their land was defeated by one vote, a vote generally credited to Sen. George Ariyoshi, now lieutenant governor. It was the beginning of an aroused Hawaiian citizenry protesting strongly, to no avail, against nonfarming leases on homestead lands and the development of Bishop Estate lands into expensive subdivisions far beyond the economic reach of most Hawaiians. A new organization, The Hawaiians, under the spiritual leadership of Reverend Akaka, has become increasingly militant, even to the extent of strongly opposing the appointment of a Japanese trustee to the Bishop Estate.

• • •

The "aloha spirit" in Hawaii is not racial. It is simply a difference in life-style emphasized by most visitors who are probably strangers to each other in their own backyard. If they would deign to smile on strangers in their hometown, considerable "aloha spirit" would be generated across the nation without having to buy an airline ticket. The visitor to Hawaii encounters an outgoing social environment—informal, without obvious traditional rules—and drops his guard against strangers. To befriend a stranger becomes the natural thing to do. Local people

The Kingdom of Hawaii's palace and gilded throne room are still maintained for the visitor to see. The throne room is a symbol of Hawaii's own nationalism, spoken of in terms of "racial mix" or "*aloha* spirit," but Hawaii's politics are pure middle class.

• • •

Hawaii's new middle class shows its muscle when environmentalists enter the political scene to challenge reckless economic growth. Today's Oriental businessman and politician is in all probability the son of an immigrant laborer. His newly won prestige in the once exclusively white social, economic, and political island community is of his own making. He is now in the seat of power, and the opportunity for wealth and influence is within striking distance. The Oriental is the advocate of conservative dress when colorful *mu'umu'u* and *aloha* shirts are proper for almost every occasion. The white businessman fosters support for "*Aloha* shirt Friday," while the Oriental executive and politician stays with his stuffy dark coat and tie, symbolizing his middle-class status. It is his turn to subdivide, develop, rise all the way in the profession of his choice, build hotels and apartments, and enjoy the profits and standards of living denied his parents in old Hawaii. He is not about to be denied by conservationists the benefits of his long struggle to the top. The land and economic growth are his future, and he will wring the profits from his islands in collaboration with the old economic oligarchy and corporate absentee owners of hotels and airlines, regardless of the consequences.

His children, now high school graduates and university freshmen, are the new Hawaii activists. They warn of get-rich-quick profits detrimental to Hawaii's future. They caution that Hawaii's fragile scenic beauty and unique island environment are the only base for a prosperous future—the irreplaceable treasure of a multimillion-dollar tourist industry inviting 2 million visitors a year to the Hawaiian Islands. A way of life is threatened. It is the young peoples' turn tomorrow.

The children of a new race are the happiest because they see tomorrow. In Hawaii, where May Day is Lei Day and the garland of flowers is a symbol of love and aloha, children surely represent the spirit of an island land—an ideal for a nation to follow.

Hawaii is the home of shanghaied men and women, who were induced to remain, not by a blow with a club over the head or a doped bottle of whisky, but by love. Hawaii and the Hawaiians are a land and a people loving and lovable. By their language may ye know them, and in what other land save this one is the commonest form of greeting, not "Good day," nor "How d'ye do," but "Love"? That greeting is Aloha—love, I love you, my love to you. Good day—what is it more than an impersonal remark about the weather? How do you do—it is personal in a merely casual interrogative sort of way. But Aloha! It is a positive affirmation of the warmth of one's own heart-giving. My love to you! I love you! Aloha!

—Jack London

Rosie Alvaro is Hawaiian, Chinese, Caucasian, and several other ethnic fractions. She personifies the neo-Hawaiian race, born of island parents at the crossroads of the Pacific, where immigrants from the Old World, Polynesia, and Asia met to love and live, and where people boast of their differences and share a world of cultures.

Molokai

Friendly Island

The coconut grove of Kamehameha V is a reminder that Molokai also enjoyed the visits of royalty. Ancient battlefield sites and heiau attest to Molokai's important role in unifying the islands as Kamehameha I battled rival chiefs from each island to establish the Kingdom of Hawaii.

IT WAS TYPICAL of Molokai. A two-page ad in the local tabloid made no exceptions—"everyone" was invited to the grand opening of Pau Hana Inn. The new hotel management invited all, and on opening night it appeared that everyone came.

The crowd was mixed. There was the manager from the competing Hotel Molokai down the road, Jimmie Moikeha, singing beautiful Hawaiian songs for his supper of *imu* pig, *kāmano lomi* (rubbed salmon), and BBQ ribs washed down with local Primo beer. Hippie couples with beards and no bras took over a long table near the free food. Part-Hawaiians in work-dirty jeans and Orientals from the Del Monte plantation danced to local music groups, while a white-haired patriarch of the Cooke family spoke glowingly of Molokai's new hotel for the "local people."

The Cooke family owned the land and half of Molokai as well. They gladly offered a lease far below market value, enabling the hotel to offer rooms and a bar with prices anyone could afford. Pau Hana Inn would not cater to the tourist. Its name, meaning "end of the day's work," invited the pineapple-truck driver to stop by and offered the *kama'āina* executive a place to forsake Honolulu for a weekend away from Waikiki's resort bustle and plastic world. The only people missing from the opening party were tourists. Molokai didn't care.

Music Hawaiian style—guitars and ukuleles—was by the "Family Five," the Dudoit family and a couple of neighborhood friends,

living far south of Kaunakakai, where the narrow dirt road to Halawa Valley winds steeply upward into Puu O Hoku ranchlands.

The road was being paved, but gaps remained. Dudoit, always alert for opportunities available to road-working crews on Molokai, called to his friends at the party for "a good lunch when I pave pass your house." An affirmative promise was made for the dirt road still remaining.

No one drove in from remote Halawa Valley, inaccessible in wet weather except for four-wheel-drive vehicles, and it is just as well. Visiting Halawa—embraced under a jungle canopy barely hiding the ruins of ancient taro patches and house sites—is a brief return to a hundred years ago. Two slender falls streak the valley wall, their waters pounding into rock-rimmed pools. A squirming stream carries the mountain water seaward, the roar of falling water barely smothered in the mango forest before the white ocean surf sounds its own challenge to the quiet valley. The road to Halawa must never be paved. Halawa will remain a place of escape as long as the road to get there stays rough.

Councilman E. Loy Cluney, speaking at the hotel dedication, must have been referring to the Halawa treasure when he remarked that "Progress is slow on Molokai. That is good. On the other islands we've seen progress. They're making so much progress in Waikiki everyone suffers." One knew without asking that Councilman Cluney lived on Molokai.

The eighty-three-year-old local pastor and self-proclaimed Hawaiian "mayor" of Molokai gave the benediction. He praised the owner; blessed the building, the parking lot, and the kitchen; and recited the Lord's Prayer. A green leaf *maile lei* stretched across the entryway was untied in the traditional manner, and the first guests crowded inside for free drinks.

Behind the bar, plastic orchids and ferns covered a black lava wall. At the front desk more fake blooms brightened the room. The *haole* hotel entrepreneur from Honolulu celebrated the event by wearing a traditional *lei* of *kukui* nuts—made of black plastic.

His guests brought gifts of growing plants and ferns, potted orchids and bright anthurium. Soon the plastic world was overwhelmed by the real world of Molokai. Workers from Maunaloa village in the middle of pineapple fields on Molokai's dry side carried in whole sections of their gardens. If anyone possessed an orderly hotel landscaping plan it was quickly forgotten as the exotic plant mix carried from across the island and down the street accumulated in the lobby.

Guests came from along the road beyond Pukoo, where Father Damien built his first

church and early Hawaiians harvested mullet for the chiefs from fishponds built a thousand years ago.

They came from Kalae and the Hawaiian Homestead lands at Hoolehua, on the windswept north side. Some walked the short distance from Kaunakakai, where merchants noticed a sudden exodus from paying bars.

Workers in the Kalaupapa leper settlement rode up the steep trail to the *pali* rim at Palaau Park, temporarily traded their horses for a Datsun parked in the fenced pasture, and coasted downhill across the island to Pau Hana Inn. Others piled into dusty pickups from Kualapuu, the company pineapple town. And more people came from Kamalo, down the coast.

As the people of Molokai swarmed through the new Pau Hana lobby, emptied the ice tubs of Primo beer, and threw aside the cleaned bones of pig and fish, they echoed the excitement of native feasts a hundred years past. The Hawaiian monarchy lived again that night. Old days returned for a moment and all Molokai remembered.

Molokai is perhaps fortunate in having been missed by most tourists and, until recently, forgotten by the land developers. Molokai's history has generally been spoken of only in terms of the Kalaupapa leper settlement and personal sacrifices of the famed Belgian priest, Father Damien, who died of leprosy contracted while ministering to his exiled patients. Released patients, slightly disfigured by the dread disease, now guide tourists around the historic peninsula on Molokai's north shore. Taboos still exist. Visitors cannot remain overnight, and it is the only place in Hawaii where walking barefooted is forbidden.

Until recent years Molokai could not advertise a modern hotel—there were none. U-Drive cars were equally scarce—only Ernest Uu rented a few—and they didn't accumulate much mileage. Every road on the entire island outside of locked gates could be driven before lunch. Travel agents seldom recommended the island, and only local deer hunters and campers from Honolulu knew of the wild valleys carved from the north shore in ancient geologic times.

The wild valleys of Molokai—Waikolu, Pelekunu, Wailau, Papalaua, and Halawa—represent the flank of a great eroded volcano, long since dormant. The great amphitheater valleys, all wider at their heads, carry large streams to the sea and support exotic jungles of taro, banana, sugarcane, and sweet potato.

Large Hawaiian populations once called these valleys home. Extensive walls of terraced taro plots and numerous house platforms testify to the existence of flourishing village life many years ago. Pelekunu claimed a few in-

habitants as recently as 1935, when the tiny post office closed. No physical evidence of the village remains, save for the rocky landing often swept by high seas.

High swampy plateaus between the deep valleys are unexplored. The upland bogs overflow during rainsqualls, sending hundreds of waterfalls cascading a half-mile down to the sea. Sometimes winds blow the tumbling water back into the sky. At Wailau so much water enters the winter ocean that swimmers drink the surf.

The ancient Hawaiian forest along the high mountain crest is dying. Mile after mile of gaunt skeletons, remnants of proud *'ōhi'a* and *koa* trees scar the isolated ridge above Wailau and Pelekunu valleys. Gnarled patriarchs remain of a once great native forest, most of them punctured with dry rot—dying and diseased trees—festooned with parasitic passion fruit vines and choked with sticky molasses grass that even the deer won't touch. Axis deer, introduced to satisfy hunters who kill for the fun of it, eat the seedlings of the dying forest. Young trees never grow. The native forests of Molokai slowly disappear like the people who once lived in the valleys. Like the Hawaiian people themselves.

The wild valleys of Molokai are not forgotten—they haven't been found yet.

The main street of Kaunakakai is a wonderful step back into a generation ago, when the pedestrian was king, parking meters did not exist, and traffic lights were unheard of. Kaunakakai is still like that.

HALAWA VALLEY

ORCHIDS

MOLOKAI PALI, NORTH SHORE

An island does not end at a wave-splashed rocky shore or along the spine of a tree-fringed ridge. An island reaches into the sea and sky, beyond the horizon and even beneath the ocean into the undersea world.

PAILOLO CHANNEL

The People & the Land Are Hawaii

THE HISTORY OF HAWAII may be told in the lives of alien men from strange worlds who fell in love with the land, and the island life-style, as they did with the Polynesian women.

Sugar baron Claus Spreckels arrived in Maui from San Francisco before the signatures on the Reciprocity Treaty of 1875 with the Kingdom of Hawaii were dry. The treaty provided for duty-free admission of sugar and fifteen other Hawaiian agricultural products into the United States. Potential profits quickly spawned across the islands a network of tiny sugar plantations developed by Americans still moving west.

Spreckels' scheming with King Kalakaua and the prime minister grew to scandalous proportions as he organized a huge sugar growing and milling combine. The wild scramble for cane land and water rights, intensified by the treaty, seriously compromised the island kingdom, which had been slowly evolving into a Pacific nation. Spreckels and other planters manipulated the crown with the same ease that they talked the Hawaiian native out of his last tiny plot of taro land. Hawaiians refused to work the fields when pigs and fish were available for the taking. They saw little incentive for adopting the daily regimentation of a wage system, so the planters' machetes were swung more and more by imported contract labor.

Hawaiian culture slowly weakened and the language was heard less and less as the native trees and plants were replaced with cane. As swiftly as Chinese stores appeared, Japanese shops followed, selling goods imported from the homeland and distributing publications printed in the strange calligraphy of the Far East. Portuguese followed the Japanese in the tidal surge of immigration from overseas. They invented the ukulele for the Hawaiians. Shiploads of Japanese continued to arrive, encouraged by sugar planters who were reaping growing profits from the cheap labor. But the planters were criticized by many fellow whites who feared the "yellow invasion," and Orientals were excluded by them from advancement and social life within the *haole* (white) community. During King Kalakaua's regime, as "asiatics," the Chinese and Japanese were prohibited from voting. The Japanese responded by establishing their own language schools and publishing, in 1892, the first Japanese newspaper.

Before the turn of the century, remote outside island communities enjoyed weekly steamer service. One early visitor in 1880 even suggested the small sugar town of Huelo on East Maui as a "good site for a tourist hotel operation." The fare from Honolulu, on Oahu, was attractive enough: a cabin for six dollars one way, the open deck, two dollars.

The reciprocity boom also brought failure to overextended sugar pioneers. In many areas the investors were forced to stop the clearing and planting of land before the first crop was harvested, when skittish stockholders failed to pay their installment assessments.

Hamoa Plantation on Maui never did pay a dividend to its founders, who, after struggling valiantly for twenty losing months, simply abandoned the land and walked away, leaving the mill to crumble into ruin. Nearby Hana Plantation picked up the pieces.

Correspondence at the time reveals that Hana and Hamoa had not been on the best of terms, with continual disagreements over water rights, roadways, leased land, and cattle. Typical of their frequently strained relations was a minor incident involving a borrowed bucket. The Hamoa manager wrote his richer neighbor requesting him to "please always return the tin pail used for the butter, so we need not buy a new one all the time."

Even though some ventures had failed, other investors thought they had a chance to succeed. Captain T. K. Clarke, skipper of the schooner *Pueokahi,* on regular runs between Honolulu and Maui, sailed often along the Kipahulu and Kaupo shores, which then were undeveloped and had remote Hawaiian villages. As early as 1874 he asked the king for permission to lease these fabled lands of Maui's Kahikinui region to grow cane; but his request was denied because natives in large numbers still lived upon the land.

In his search for virgin land to develop, Clarke met W. B. Starkey, husband of the Hawaiian Chieftess Kehele, living in Kipahulu. Together they formed a partnership, and in 1880 Clarke left his ship in Hana Bay and rode on horseback overland to try his luck as a sugar planter. With his partner, he first constructed a masonry landing convenient to the proposed mill site and, as the small coastal schooner *Mokolii* began regular calls, hauled ashore tons of equipment for cultivating and milling.

Several coastal schooners maintained good communications between Honolulu and the landings at Nuu, Kaupo, Kipahulu, Maalaea, Hamoa, and the layover port of Hana. The tiny vessels were loaded offshore by bouncing whaleboats ferrying the valuable sugar and molasses from the rocky landings, constantly awash from spray stirred by the long channel swells. They returned with provisions of all kinds to stock the company store and to supply parts for the mills that were grinding out raw, golden sugar. Coal, lumber, dry goods, and food from across the seas were carried by muleback to the busy sugar towns. Most passengers traveled on deck with the carousing Hawaiians who laughed, chatted,

smoked, ate *poi* from common bowls, and drank themselves insensible.

Departing from Kipahulu the coastal steamers stopped offshore at Kaupo, where cargo was still ferried to surf-swept landings and hauled ashore on stiff-legged timber hoists, cranked by husky Hawaiians who plucked the burlap-wrapped freight from wildly bouncing longboats.

The pioneering land gave birth to rugged individualists who thrived on adversity. Isolated by geography and by primitive transportation from city social life and urban sources of supply, ingenuity became a byword for their survival. The merchant or planter who was not self-sufficient and inventive soon departed. Those who remained carried on the tough traditions of the early Hawaiians, but by now they were multiracial nationals from around the world.

The young man, Nick Soon, watching his supplies being swung ashore at Kaupo's Mokulau landing met every boat to pick up stock for the Look Kee store at Kaupo, southernmost of the chain of Chinese stores owned by his merchant father, a companion of Chinese patriot Sun Yat-sen. Nick's eight mules, at times loaded with 300 pounds of rice each, carefully trod the narrow trail up from the rocky landing, making countless round trips of one mile to the store in Kaupo village, little more than a ranch outpost and gathering place for the few remaining Hawaiian families scattered across Kahikinui, who still lived in the grass huts that were fast disappearing throughout the islands.

Nick's family had arrived in Hawaii with the early imported Chinese plantation contract workers, but, like most Chinese, they found little to be gained by rioting against the white bosses. Instead they left the plantation as quickly as possible, many establishing small trading stores in remote areas, planting rice, and, in a few localities, creating small communities as they married native girls and settled down to grow taro for the Hawaiians. Chinese traditionally held ownership of land to be important, calling land "living property." Royal land grants held by Hawaiian women married to Chinese were seldom split up and sold off to sugar-land agents.

Nick Soon personally operated the family store in Kipahulu, directly across from the mill. He was also the postmaster and chef at his small "coffee shop" next door, serving tea and Chinese cakes along with a local version of Hawaiian "chop suey."

Services provided by Nick grew with the needs of relatively isolated Kipahulu and Kaupo. When the first watches appeared, he learned how to repair them. Many years later he became the only radio repairman within a

hundred miles. He took the first photographs of Kipahulu at the turn of the century, teaching himself how to develop the film and fix proofing-out paper exposed in the sun. Hawaiians, gathered outside his store in bright sunlight for family portraits, were surprised one day when he displayed a model airplane that flew almost the length of the Kipahulu millyard. It was their first glimpse of a flying machine, but Nick was to give the local populace an even greater thrill when he brought the first car ashore in Kaupo, a 1916 Ford Model T. There were only one and a half miles of road in Kaupo at the time.

Several years later when he planned to buy a Ford Model T pickup, he discovered the old wooden derrick at Mokulau was not capable of lifting the new, heavier vehicle. No roads then reached Kaupo, but Nick Soon was not discouraged. Maintaining his first automobile had made him a skilled mechanic, so he methodically purchased all the separate parts he needed from eight different companies: the frame, seats, fenders, body, engine parts. He bought the bare engine block from the Kahului store and winched everything ashore at Kaupo, where he carefully assembled the parts in the backyard of the new general store constructed by himself the year before. It ran well.

One night the elder Kahikinui Hawaiians were bewildered by a strange light in the Kaupo store, a white light that did not flicker

or fade during the evening. Nick Soon had built for his Edison light a generator powered by his old Ford motor—the first electricity in Kaupo and Kipahulu.

A man of another world who shared tea and cakes at Nick Soon's Kipahulu coffee shop was Sentaro Ishii, a samurai from Japan. Almost six feet tall, unusual for a Japanese, he was handsome in appearance and regal in his walk.

Sentaro was trained in Japan from birth as a samurai warrior. Discharged by his lord, Sentaro disgustedly threw his samurai sword into the river in Bizen, Japan, and set out on his own. Refusing to marry the daughter of the family who had adopted him in Tokyo, he signed a labor contract for plantation work in Hawaii after being told of the great opportunities working in the cane fields at four dollars a month. He agreed it was a splendid offer and sailed from Yokohama on a Spanish ship captained by an American.

Arriving in Hawaii, Sentaro labored three years in the high, upland sugar fields of Maui. "I had never farmed in my life," he said in later years. "My profession was to fight with the sword." Sentaro bought his first shirt and pants at the company store.

Captain James Makee, a retired ship's master and owner of the Rose Plantation had taught the eager Japanese immigrant how to cook. When Makee's friend Captain Clarke had

gone into the sugar business, Makee gave him the new cook, so Sentaro took the coastal steamer around the island to Kipahulu and worked as a cook and personal servant for the new plantation manager.

The first Japanese contract workers for Kipahulu arrived without a translator, and Sentaro was pulled out of the kitchen to work again in the fields. This time he went to work astride a horse, overseeing the new laborers. He could speak English and was fluent in both Hawaiian and Japanese, making him invaluable as a field *luna*.

The plantation shortly settled into a routine of planting, harvesting, and milling, but profits were hard to come by. Barely six years after the first cane was planted, Clarke died. His partner, W. B. Starkey, became disenchanted with Hawaiian plantation life, sold his interest, and, leaving his Hawaiian wife behind, sailed home to England.

At the age of sixty-one, Sentaro, never having married, wooed and won for his first bride, Kehele Starkey, wife of the former plantation manager. She owned most of the private land of Kipahulu and was twenty years his junior. Friends at the Catholic wedding said Sentaro also looked twenty years younger. He called his Hawaiian wife *Take* (the Japanese word for bamboo), and later named his two sons and two daughters after the plum and pine—in the classical samurai tradition—the trees of happiness and longevity.

With Clarke and Starkey gone, the German sugar agency of Hackfeld and Company in Honolulu gradually acquired controlling interest in the English-owned firm. Sentaro was never fully accepted as a part of management.

Another field overseer was hired, a Chinese from Puunene in the Maui flatlands, who worked with the Japanese Sentaro in a unique arrangement duplicated nowhere else in the predominantly white Hawaiian sugar establishment.

The new *luna*, Ah Ping, was a contract laborer from Los Angeles who had left China when he was a young man. His previous contract employers refused to return him to California when their Molokai sugar plantation failed and, like Sentaro, he had left the fields and learned to cook, and then worked in private homes before taking a coastal schooner to Kipahulu.

The new owners hired German nationals to manage operations. They quickly proved unsuited to the primitive life of Kipahulu. The first, a Mr. Barekhausen, returned to the city life of Honolulu before twelve months had passed. His successor, Mr. Buckholtz, also departed before the next humid summer. The third German manager, Mr. Gross, lasted longer, but he and the Chinese *luna* did not

get along, so Ah Ping packed his bags and left to work for the new Pioneer mill on the dry side of the island at Lahaina.

In 1906, the small plantation was in poor financial condition, due mostly to frequent changes in executives, and a new manager, Mr. Haneberg, was hired in the hope that the fortunes of Kipahulu would be restored, but Haneberg was unable to reverse the downward trend. The plantation returned no profits to its owners, despite valiant efforts.

Meeting in Honolulu the desperate German board of directors for the Hackfeld company (now Amfac) proposed a then unheard-of solution to their problems. The suggestion was to hire Ah Ping as plantation manager! The majority strongly objected to hiring a Chinese, saying that only white men could be trusted in such an important position and that the white mill engineer would refuse to work for a "Chinaman."

But Ah Ping's credentials were impressive. He could speak English, Hawaiian, and Chinese. White overseers in Lahaina spoke highly of his skills. When Haneberg asked for a $1,000 raise, the directors stopped their debate and hired the Chinese, but not without taking the precaution of first contracting for a white "inspector" to watch over him, which

almost doubled the wages they would have paid Haneberg alone.

With Sentaro in the fields as head *luna* and Ah Ping in the office, Kipahulu sugar began to return a small profit. It was the only plantation in Hawaii ever to be managed by an Oriental, and Ah Ping proved the directors' judgment to be excellent. The federal Alien Property Custodian confiscated the assets of the Hackfeld company at the outbreak of World War I, but the Germans had sold Kipahulu at a good price to the American Fassoth family from Kauai shortly before the war started and so Kipahulu escaped.

The new owners replaced most of Kipahulu's staff with their own family, and Ah Ping retired to Molokai, where he operated a small general store along the shore road south of Kaunakakai.

Martin Fassoth became chemist and mill superintendent; Joseph, head bookkeeper; Hans worked in the fields as a *luna;* and John Jr. was the timekeeper. Fassoth modernized the mill and installed new evaporators and mill rollers.

Interned German aliens were sent to Kipahulu in 1917, and Fassoth utilized their skills to build a new chimney for the mill, the first concrete smokestack on Maui. A theater was

ONELOA BEACH AND PINEAPPLE FIELDS, MAUI

constructed, and movies were shown once a week, the film coming in by wagon over the new road.

The plantation boasted of 300 employees, mostly Chinese and Japanese, who lived in the growing Kipahulu village clustered around the mill. Kipahulu was without a hotel, but overnight travelers were fed well in Nick Soon's coffee shop, and on rainy evenings slept in the warm boilerhouse. Leaving early in the morning, visitors generally stopped at the flimsy wooden girder bridge spanning Oheo Stream outside of town to wash in the cool Seven Pools strung like beads above and below the narrow road to Hana.

The price of sugar skyrocketed during World War I; before the armistice was signed, high profits paid off Fassoth's purchase price. His health suffered, and when he died the family sold the 2,800 cultivated acres. The land was then used for growing pineapples. The last sugar was harvested in 1923, when the Fassoth brothers dismantled the mill and shipped it to Manila. But it rained too much at Kipahulu for pineapple, and after two years of losses the depression ended dreams of a fortune from pineapple.

Upon hearing the news, Maui's Baldwin family acquired the cleared land and implemented plans to transform the old plantation land into a working cattle ranch. What was too small for sugar and too wet for pineapple was just right for ranching. At Kipahulu the cattle would enjoy year-round green pastures to supplement their extensive acreage on the dry north slopes of Haleakala.

Within weeks the first cattle were unloaded at the Kipahulu landing on the rocky south shore and herded up the grassy slopes past the remains of the German chimney, now standing alone amid piles of broken red brick behind the old mill. The restless cattle were corralled by yelling Hawaiian cowboys, excited by their new domain.

Turning away from the intruders, Nick Soon quietly closed the doors of his coffee shop for the last time. His associate across the street shuttered the windows of his store. Ten cowboys would take care of ranchlands where 300 people once labored in sugar and pineapple fields.

Wagons were loaded with household furniture, carefully packed family treasures, and laughing children unaware of the tragedy. People with bewildered expressions mixed with streaming tears crowded the narrow main street of Kipahulu—no longer a town—as departing residents whipped their horses up the road toward Hana and a new home. Others walked sadly down the easy grade to the Kipahulu landing, replacing cattle off-loaded that morning from the waiting black-hulled steamer tossing gently in the rough channel swells. Entire families, born and raised on the small plantation, left forever the trim whitewashed cottages framed behind low picket fences along the dusty paths, their carefully tended flowers blooming brightly. Behind them an occasional cowboy family moved into a still-warm house.

Sentaro Ishii stayed in Kipahulu, where he lived to be 102 years old. Nick Soon still lives in the country store at Kaupo. They are part of the Hawaiian tradition—the stories of visitors to Hawaii who fell in love with the islands and remained to live their lives on a beautiful land.

PARKER RANCH, MAUNA KEA, HAWAII

How To Kill a Forest

ISTORIANS TRACE the origin of the Hawaiian sandalwood trade to Capt. John Kendrick, master of the American clipper *Lady Washington,* and to Capt. William Douglas, of the schooner *Grace,* in 1791—just thirteen years after Captain Cook's landing in 1778. The first real impact of sandalwood trading was not to be felt on the Big Island of Hawaii, however, until about 1810. In 1812, at the beginning of the war with England, three Bostonians—Jonathan and Nathan Winship and William Heath Davis—exercised their Yankee shrewdness by signing an agreement with Kamehameha I for a ten-year exclusive monopoly in the export of island sandalwood. John Palmer Parker, later founder of the Parker Ranch, was a crewman in their fleet bound for Canton, China, in 1812.

(A sidelight regarding the intelligence and diplomatic aplomb of the fierce-appearing Kamehameha I rates mention here. In 1812, so goes the tale, while Great Britain and the United States were at war, Kamehameha was justifiably anxious to continue trade and friendly relations with both these powerful countries. In order to better protect his fleet on the high seas, to encourage a continuance of trade between tiny Hawaii and the warring powers, and to keep the French and Russians wary, he helped design an ingenious flag—a compromise flag utilizing the Union Jack of the British and the stripes similar to those of America's Old Glory. Today that same flag is the state flag of Hawaii.)

The agreement of the Winships and Davis with Kamehameha stipulated that the king would have the sandalwood gathered and waiting for their ships. They would sail the wood to Chinese ports, sell it, and upon return, give Kamehameha his share—one-quarter of their net profit. The war and the blockading of the ships in Canton by the British abrogated this exclusive contract.

Other traders, including John Jacob Astor of New York, found the sandalwood trade appealing and entered the wide-open market. The sandalwood tree soon became the most valued commodity of the Hawaiian economy.

Sandalwood, called *'ili-ahi,* is a parasite that attaches itself to the root of another tree, and as it grows it becomes a super hard, highly fragrant wood. It is still in great demand in Asia, where it is used as incense, fuel for funeral rites, for carved temple idols and hand-carved boxes, in medicine, and as a basic ingredient in perfume. Sandalwood became the main source of revenue for almost all of Hawaii's royalty. The rush that followed made it appear that a Comstock lode of wood had been discovered, that a few "savages" owned it, and that it was there for any shrewd trader who could supply a seaworthy ship and crew.

The list of items traded for sandalwood included beads, schooners, silks, rifles, rum, cut glass, wool suits, pistols, party dresses, cutlasses, billiard tables, mirrors, cannons. Many items traded had no practical use in the islands. These goods, under armed guard, rotted in dank caves and humid grass shacks.

One writer of the time explained:

"It was through sandalwood that slavery replaced freedom to the people. Natives were treated like cattle. Up and down the treacherous mountain trails they toiled, logs of sandalwood strapped to their sweating shoulders. Men and women actually became deformed due to the tremendous weight of the logs on their backs. The forced laborers in the sandalwood forests had no time to farm—food grew scarce and famine came."

After nine years of ruling his kingdom from Oahu, Kamehameha returned to Kailua village on the Kona coast of his beloved Big Island in 1812 and noted the hardship that sandalwood trading was inflicting on his subjects. Many were physically deformed, and others were helplessly starving to death. As some small recompense for the suffering that the royal greed had caused his loyal followers, Kamehameha immediately put his court of indolent chiefs to laboring in taro and sweet potato patches, and as an example for others to follow, he returned to the land himself and began farming a field in Kailua. He refused to eat produce from any other source. Upon Kamehameha's death seven years later, sandalwood trading expanded and continued unchecked, and soon it brought all of Hawaii to the brink of a great disaster.

Those New England traders who swarmed to Hawaii to profit from sandalwood suffered from a financial crisis at home and demanded payment on promissory notes held against island chiefs. When the chiefs asked for more time to pay, these traders complained vociferously to the United States government that missionaries were interfering with business by occupying the time and utilizing the energy of the Hawaiian people in religious services, school attendance, and the building of churches. In 1826, during the administration of President John Quincy Adams, whose secretary of state was Henry Clay, the United States government responded to the pleas of the profit-taking traders by sending two American warships to the islands to "render all possible aid to American commerce."

Although the sandalwood forests were almost denuded by 1831, most debts owed by Hawaiian chiefs to American traders were paid during that year or rewritten for payment by 1843. Thus ended the sandalwood chapter in Hawaiian history. Today, only a few sandalwood trees still grow in Hawaii.

A well-maintained state highway—from the conservationist's point of view.

PUUIKI, NEAR KIPAHULU, MAUI

GOLDEN TREE, OAHU

CORAL TREE, KAUAI

BANYAN TREE, MOLOKAI

TORCH GINGER, OAHU

'AMA'UMA'U FERN, KAUAI

BIRD-OF-PARADISE, LANAI

TIGERS CLAW, HAWAII ISLAND

PLUMERIA

CUP OF GOLD

VANDA ORCHIDS

Lanai

Pineapple Island

WILD PINEAPPLE

Lanai City is the image of a company town set in a Midwest landscape, but the tall trees are pines from Norfolk Island near Australia, and the most common vehicles are surplus military Jeeps. Central heating in the small brightly painted homes is unknown. It is seldom chilly on Lanai.

WHILE THE STATE LEGISLATURE debates the issue of an optimum population for Hawaii and ecologists predict the eventual collapse of Hawaii's fabled life-style and economy unless population and tourism growth are soon halted, the owners of 141-square-mile Lanai Island quietly go about implementing a master plan that matter-of-factly calls for a maximum 12,500 population—including 2,000 tourists—by 1985. Today's population: 2,204. Over 80 percent of the island will remain in agriculture, open space, and forest lands.

Lanai is owned by Castle and Cooke, canners of Dole pineapple and the nation's fifth-largest food processing corporation. Their wise planners have already discarded the obsolete concept of planning *ad infinitum* and are designing a quality community within the limitations of the island's natural resources, water supply, agricultural jobs, tourist potential, and recreational opportunities. They are designing for a quality life-style.

The planning team has decided that Lanai's only town, Lanai City, will remain the only town, picturesquely sited on the upland shelf where the only mountain, Lanaihale, begins. Lanai City resembles a mainland town, with tall, firlike Norfolk Island evergreen pines casting long shadows across repetitive grid blocks holding small plantation cottages that boast of the most colorful front yards to be seen anywhere. Higher on the hillside perch larger homes for plantation supervisors. In the

highest and largest house lives the plantation manager. While Lanai City is still a company town to the eye, its social structure is rapidly changing, as new job opportunities appear.

All of Lanai's paved roads end in four-wheel-drive tracks, elevating the surplus military jeep to second-car status and mandating tourists to dust and mud if they want to leave town. No road encircles the island—not even a trail—and the venturesome visitor quickly learns the technique of shifting into compound low gear and dodging thorny *kiawe* tree branches along the shore.

Shipwreck Beach on the windward shore opposite Molokai is a graveyard of old ships stranded on the shallow reef and scattered across tidal flats. Winter storms continue to batter the broken hulks into submission, and barely recognizable hulks of old sailing vessels litter the beach. Early risers walk the windy beach searching for treasure in the drifting flotsam.

King Kamehameha I maintained a favorite summer fishing hut on the beach at Kaunolu, where eighty-six house platforms and thirty-five stone shelters scattered around the scenic area attest to a well-populated village at one time. Now a national historic landmark, the site includes *Halulu Heiau* (temple) dominating the rocky promontory near Kahekili's Jump, where candidates for Kamehameha's personal entourage are said to have demonstrated their courage by leaping into the sea from a sixty-two-foot-high cliff, springing far out to miss the protruding rocky shelf directly below. Those who succeeded joined the king. Failures contributed to the successful fishing that the isolated point is still noted for.

Hawaiian girls who committed adultery were banished to an early penal colony set up by the king on the northwest Lanai coast, an arrangement which apparently worked out quite well for the male criminals banished to nearby Kahoolawe Island. Stories are told of escapades when male prisoners stopped by Lanai to pick up their girls for the weekend before raiding the nearby Makena vegetable gardens on Maui.

Protestant missionaries first held services on Lanai in 1835. Mormon leader Walter Murray Gibson arrived about twenty years later and started a church colony, inviting Hawaiians to join him again in communal living and polygamy that the natives had abandoned before the other missionaries came. Hawaiians gave him their land, and Gibson purchased extensive cattle-grazing acreage with church money. The colony flourished but Salt Lake authorities eventually closed down the operation when Gibson refused to deed his land acquisitions to the church. Gibson eventually became a confidant of King Kalakaua while his

converts sailed for Salt Lake City, where a small Hawaiian colony still thrives.

Few native plants survive anywhere. Even the lofty profile of 3,370-foot-high Lanaihale is outlined with imported Norfolk Island pines planted from horseback by an early ranch manager-naturalist to collect moisture from low clouds that hug the mountain summit every afternoon.

Most of Lanai is covered with impenetrable thickets of phreatophytes—*kiawe, koa-haole,* and tamarisk—trees that drain the soil of water and give Lanai its arid appearance. The Lanai company has a solution: they plan to bulldoze out the water parasites and replant the entire island with substitute plants which suck up less water. Lanai may look a little different fifty years from now with an ecological change of this magnitude. But then Lanai has always taken new introductions in its stride.

It was in the dry *kiawe-pā-nini* forest of Palawai Basin before pineapple was planted that Lanai experienced its first automobile accident many years ago. The only two cars on the island collided head-on.

KAHEKILI'S JUMP AT KAUNOLU

The folklore of Hawaii tells how Lanai was in-habited only by evil spirits and ghosts long after Polynesians settled neighboring Maui Is-land. When Kahekili, the ruling chief of Maui, discovered his sister was unable to discipline her mischievous son, Kaululaau, he was ban-ished to Lanai for punishment. No one ex-pected him to survive, but he fought the ghosts hand-to-hand and eventually made Lanai a safe place for human beings to live. In later years the island was used as a penal colony for women who were banished to Lanai from the kingdom for committing adultery.

THE WATER AT MANELE

107 PINEAPPLE ISLAND

Lanaihale (house of Lanai), a mountain 3,370 feet high, was reforested many years ago with imported temperate zone trees to replace native forests ravaged by feral goats and pigs. Imported deer and antelope continue the destruction of native seedlings while offering unusual hunting opportunities to local sportsmen. A sign near the terminal building at Lanai's small airport claims that the 15,000-acre spread on Lanai under cultivation by Dole Corporation is the "world's largest pineapple plantation." Handpicked with the help of complex harvesting machines, ripe fruit is shipped by barge to the Honolulu cannery for processing.

109 PINEAPPLE ISLAND

. . . to the proposition that never was so much climate gathered together in one place, can be added that never was so much landscape gathered together in one place.

—*Jack London*

MANELE BEACH, SUNRISE

MAUI ISLAND FROM SUMMIT OF LANAIHALE, SUNRISE

HILO BAY, AROUND 1900, AND TODAY

The Heritage of an Island People

SUBDUE AND CONQUER THE EARTH. The Judeo-Christian ethic hailing the conquest of nature as a virtue may have received a setback in Hawaii. The early Polynesians, finding a home in Hawaii after arduous outrigger canoe voyages across the open ocean from Tahiti and Samoa, hardly considered technology and materialism the sole objectives of mankind. The long trip to Hawaii was made to find a better place to live—an escape from oppressive rule and overpopulation.

The Polynesians' search for a new lifestyle ended in Hawaii. The 2,000 nautical miles of colder waters between Hawaii and the not yet discovered bay called San Francisco were never challenged. Hawaii became the ultimate destination: the end of a voyage begun many generations before in distant Indochina and Southeast Asia.

The pioneering Hawaiians easily solved the problems of living on an island. Without benefit of research or contemporary scientific knowledge available to the Western world, they evolved a land use system admirably suited to a finite island ecosystem. Recurrent wars of the time, human sacrifice, and prevailing infanticide seemed to provide a macabre ecological balance between population and daily needs of food and housing.

Limited natural resources were exploited in direct relation to need by a unique division of the land into *ahupua'a,* pie-shaped portions extending from the rich shore waters beyond the beach to the summit peaks deep in the island interior. All varieties of food were harvested within these parcels: the sea provided fish; lowlands grew taro in swampy waters edged by coconuts; sweet potatoes, bananas, and sugarcane flourished on the lower slopes; birds were collected upland (and released after the plucking of feathers) for royal capes. In the high mountain forests new hardwood *koa* tree seedlings were encouraged to grow for every canoe log manhandled to the shore.

All the needs of life, including fiber for tapa clothing, plentiful surface water, and palm thatch, were available to the commoner, who did, however, live at the pleasure of the chief. There were generally sufficient surpluses to pay the chief annual taxes in breadfruit, *lau hala* mats, and pigs. The commoner willingly went to battle for the chief to defend the *ahupua'a* and preserve a way of life seemingly unassailable. The life was not a paradise, yet there were considerable advantages over contemporary European serfdom. For one, the weather was warmer.

These, then, were the islands—missed by Ferdinand Magellan and Sir Francis Drake—that the ubiquitous Capt. James Cook finally stumbled upon in 1778 and which he named the Sandwich Islands. At that time Hawaiian culture was already over 1,500 years old. Language and culture born of an isolated native autocracy were already a part of legend and chant.

Cook carved out the Pacific for his domain, and his discoveries unloosed a wave of Western ideas and a European colonialism in the Pacific that placed all the islands under a foreign flag. Every island except Hawaii.

By accident of fate, Hawaii escaped the yoke of European colonization. While accepting the trappings of Western royalty, Hawaii resisted dominance by foreign powers, entering the nineteenth century still an independent kingdom.

Spanish admirals plundered the New World while the Hawaiian chief Kamehameha united Hawaiian islands by force into a native kingdom. Spanish galleons, on scheduled monthly voyages from Manila to Acapulco, crossed the Pacific a hundred and more times. They missed Hawaii on every trip. The vast Pacific domain pacified by Spanish Jesuits did not include the Sandwich Islands. Other Western explorers, dropping off goats and cattle for Hawaiian chiefs, never tarried long enough to write a law.

The fur-trading Russians arrived on Kauai, but hardly overawed the natives. When they began constructing forts, the Kauai chief demanded they leave. They did.

American missionaries out of Boston were welcomed. The Hawaiians had already thrown out their pagan *kapu* system of idol worship and were waiting for a replacement. The missionaries offered an acceptable religion, and the Hawaiians adopted it all. Jesus Christ was accepted with barely a murmur. Conversion was hardly a matter of proselytization—there was a gap to be filled, and American missionaries were the first to arrive.

While the political occupation of Hawaii was long delayed, economic exploitation began with the whalers, followed by the sandalwood traders, and then the missionaries. An ex-missionary convinced the Hawaiian king that private ownership of land was moral and just. Subsistence living and the *ahupua'a* disappeared with the arrival of Western sugar barons.

The first large-scale commercial sugar plantation was established on Kauai by a pioneering capitalist from California who later returned to the Bay Area and organized San Francisco's first Chamber of Commerce. Once the sugar barons became politically involved, it was a simple matter to accomplish the next step. The Hawaiian monarchy was overthrown by Americans seeking tariff reciprocity, and a republic was temporarily established to cover up a situation embarrassing to President Grover Cleveland. In predictable time the islands became the Territory of Hawaii.

Writing from Hartford, Connecticut, in 1873, Mark Twain put it well: "Now, let us annex the islands. Think how we could build up that whaling trade! Let us annex. We could make sugar enough there to supply all America, perhaps, and the prices would be very easy with the duties removed. And then we would have such a fine half-way house for our Pacific-plying ships; and such a convenient supply depot and such a commanding sentry box for an armed squadron; and we could raise cotton and coffee there and make it pay pretty well, with the duties off and capital easier to get at. And then we would own the mightiest volcano on earth—Kilauea! Barnum could run it—he understands fires now. Let us annex, by all means. We could pacify Prince Bill and other nobles easily enough—put them on a reservation. Nothing pleases a savage like a reservation—a reservation where he has his annual hoes, and bibles and blankets to trade for powder and whisky—a sweet Arcadian retreat fenced in with soldiers. By annexing, we would get all those 50,000 natives cheap as dirt, with their morals and other diseases thrown in. No expense for education—they are already educated; no need to convert them—they are already converted; no expense to clothe them—for obvious reasons.

"We *must* annex those people. We can afflict them with our wise and beneficent governments. We can introduce the novelty of thieves, all the way from street-car pickpockets to municipal robbers and government defaulters, and show them how amusing it is to arrest them and try them and then turn them loose—some for cash and some for "political influence". We can make them ashamed of their simple and primitive justice. . . . We can give them juries composed entirely of the most simple and charming leatherheads. We can give them railway corporations who will buy their legislature like old clothes, and run over their best citizens and complain of the corpses for smearing their unpleasant juices on the track. We can . . . furnish them some Jay Goulds who will do away with their old-time notion that stealing is not respectable . . . . We can give them lecturers! I will go myself.

"We can make that little bunch of sleepy islands the hottest corner on earth, and array it in the moral splendor of our high and holy civilization. Annexation is what the poor islanders need. 'Shall we to men benighted, the lamp of life deny?' "

In 1900, Hawaii became a territory of the United States.

The power system from mainland America met a new adversary in Hawaii—humanism.

Western terrestrial ambitions and search for economic profits were somehow tempered by Polynesian warmth and tolerance.

Hawaii was not without its ruthless plantation overseers. The early contractual plantation system itself was little short of slavery. Striking workers were quickly divided into racial groups fighting among themselves. Defeat was simply a matter of waiting for the Oriental to become a scab at the service of his white employers. He generally did.

Hawaiians were seldom involved. They had long since decided that working ten hours a day in the sugar fields for someone else was absurd when fish in the sea waited only for a throw net and fat boar roamed free in the hills. Hawaiians were so self-sufficient they even thatched their own houses.

In a way it was typical of Hawaii that on Sunday morning, December 7, 1941, the admiral and general in charge of United States military forces were out playing golf when Japanese imperial forces arrived in dive-bombers and torpedo planes. Hawaii was lucky the enemy was unprepared to follow up on America's unpreparedness. Probably symbolic of the whole episode were the protests of an elderly Japanese gentleman who was jerked out of an underground sewer by soldier MPs thinking they had captured a spy. He was just hiding, he said, "I was scared."

On Tuesday several army lieutenants and two mainland civilians drove southeast out of downtown Honolulu to take over the University of Hawaii for the suddenly expanded Honolulu office of the Corps of Engineers. At Punahou and Wilder streets they saw the sign, "Oahu College," and rode triumphantly into the grounds of Punahou School, the oldest private school west of the Mississippi. Two weeks later they learned the university buildings were

actually two blocks farther up the road. It was too late. The military occupied Punahou for the duration.

In the suspenseful weeks following the sneak Pearl Harbor attack, a young officer in Army Intelligence convinced local security authorities that Hawaii's Japanese were loyal to America and halted plans to exile Japanese to concentration camps on the mainland—a far better treatment than West Coast Japanese received. No act of sabotage ever occurred in Hawaii, and the officer went on to become governor.

Except for two 500-pound aerial bombs dropped in early March, the islands were not attacked again—war never returned to Hawaii. Neither did the much vaunted good old days. Hawaii was never again the same. While the economic royalists and old-style plantation politicians desperately clung to prewar traditions, the mainland *haole* (white outsiders) stayed on. They were joined by a new crop of AJAs (Americans of Japanese ancestry), who had no intention of returning to the plantations, and sugar workers who demanded changes. All had seen the other world.

Harry Bridges, of the International Longshoremen's and Warehousemen's Union, had sailed over on Matson Lines before the war to organize Hawaiian longshoremen. At the war's end, the ILWU regional director, Jack Hall, had signed up the longshoremen and virtually all sugar and pineapple plantation workers in the territory. The workers were ready. In 1946 every sugar company was struck. It was the first time in Hawaii's labor history that every race walked out together. The laborers wanted union recognition, a contract, higher wages, but probably most important, an end to the demeaning perquisite system. Instead of free housing, free hospitalization, free doctors, and

a lifetime allegiance to the plantation, they demanded cash and independence. They demanded recognition as citizens.

The sugar workers became self-sufficient during the strike. They could have held out for years. Each company town became a commune. Those who were barbers cut hair. Mechanics repaired cars. Fishermen fished. Hunters hunted. Union members with a gift of gab talked downtown merchants out of rice—distributed by the union according to need. The whole scene frightened the capitalist plantation owner—especially since the entire operation occurred on plantation property. Workers had no rent to pay—they stayed in company housing. Union strike headquarters occupied the company gymnasium. In the long bitter struggle that would make or break the union, management never evicted the workers. The plantation system in Hawaii seemed to possess hidden humanistic qualities; retribution against the workers stopped somewhat short of what might have been expected. The union won. The strike had lasted two and a half months.

The old political and economic structure died with the paternalistic plantation system. Americanization of Hawaii produced a middle-class society where none existed before—but the easygoing life-style survived. The unrestrained welcome once extended to the missionaries melded with the new imported cultures from around the world, and the "open society" became a contemporary political slogan—a simple extension of old-fashioned Hawaiian hospitality. Hawaiians accepted the best of progressive social concepts and seasoned the additions with their own island humanism they called, "aloha."

Winter storms at times mantle the highest peaks in snow, as at Mauna Kea, Hawaii. Hanauma Bay, Oahu, was the first undersea wilderness preserve in the United States. The nene goose is the state bird of Hawaii—and an endangered species. The shorescape is at Hana, Maui.

NUUANU PALI ROAD, PAST AND PRESENT, HONOLULU, OAHU

How To Kill a Tree

THE EARLY HAWAIIANS were afraid of the forest. *Menehune* and other strange creatures lived deep in the woods, and the mysteries of their nocturnal missions (the entire *Menehune* fishpond on Kauai was reputed to have been built in one night) kept the Hawaiians in their villages along the shore.

When natives did venture up the mountain to trap rare birds for the *ali'i* (chief's) feather capes or to drag out rough-hewn canoe logs, they took care to appease the gods. The birds were not killed, but carefully plucked and released to regrow more of the colored feathers prized by their chiefs. When a *koa* tree was felled, the disturbed earth was prepared so new seedlings would grow abundantly in its place.

When traders sailing out of mainland West Coast ports pointed out the profits to be made from sandalwood, native fear of upland forests disappeared. The islands were quickly stripped of sandalwood. Giant tree ferns were harvested for *pulu* to stuff the mattresses of Oriental courtesans in Cathay. Pandanus logs fueled whalers' blubber pots. Anything left after feral goats, pigs, and wild cattle rampaged across the fertile hills was fed into the boilers of a rapidly growing sugar industry.

Except in remote upland areas, little forest remained by 1900, when small villages became towns and trails were replaced by coral-surfaced streets. Hilo's street grid was reportedly laid out by survey crews sighting on a single coconut palm that grew proudly for many years in the intersection of Waiwainui and Kamehameha avenues.

The tall, slender palm was said to be the tallest in all Hawaii. While an occasional horse was tethered to its wrinkled trunk, the frond canopy was too high for any shade and too old to produce worthy coconuts. With age, grew respect, however, but when the first horseless carriage on Hilo's unpaved streets nudged the palm on a tight turn, the palm became a "traffic hazard." Its existence was threatened, so the county fathers at the behest of Hilo women's clubs enacted a protective ordinance, forbidding anyone to cut down the seemingly ageless palm under penalty of law. It may have been the first tree in Hawaii temporarily saved from the destructive hand of a traffic engineer.

Hawaii County Ordinance No. 39, effective on the first day of August, 1909, was pioneering legislation of its kind, possibly the first in the nation. The law stated quite clearly that "It shall be unlawful for any person, association, partnership or corporation . . . in any manner whatsoever to cut, trim, mutilate, destroy or appropriate any shade, ornamental, fruit, or other tree growing upon any sidewalk, highway or private property within the County of Hawaii without first having . . . permission . . . from the Board of Supervisors of the County by resolution . . . at a regular meeting. . . ." Violation was punishable by a fine of $100 or six months' imprisonment for each tree decapitated or "appropriated."

It was the expressed intention of the supervisors that permission would never be granted for felling the downtown coconut palm, and the daily *Hilo Tribune* wrote glowingly of the progressive law. In one editorial on November 16, 1909, the editors referred to growing community awareness: "A few years ago the word 'Conservation' was almost unknown, whereas now it is on every tongue. Within the last year a great wave of conservation has been passing over these Islands and there are now very few people who do not know what it means." Conservation is not a fad in Hawaii.

The same editorial went on to remind readers of the great forests that once covered Hawaii when the Polynesians first arrived. "Less than a century ago the Hawaiian Islands were densely wooded with great trees and thick underbrush. For example take Waimea [on the Parker Ranch]; eighty years ago there was a Health Station there which could not be reached except by going on a muddy trail through a wilderness of trees and underbrush dripping wet. On the Hamakua coast [sugar plantations] the forests extended down to the cliffs by the sea, and the same conditions existed on Kauai. Where . . . Honolulu is now built was once a forest of great koa trees."

The lone Hilo palm was threatened again in 1910 when the Hackfeld company, predecessor to today's Amfac, prepared plans for construction of a modern concrete office building at the intersection of Waiwainui and Kamehameha. Hackfeld officials decided to move an existing two-story wood building on the site diagonally across the street; but investigation proved there was insufficient room to go around the palm, now considered quite venerable by many Hilo residents. The contractor decided the palm must go, adding that it was a "menace to public safety."

The Hilo women's group was outraged at the news, and 140 of the ladies signed a petition addressed to the board of supervisors asking them to prevent destruction of the tree.

Hackfeld's contractor protested that the "petition was premature," adding that he had no intention of removing the tree. The county clerk subsequently wrote the Hilo women's "congress" on February 9. "I have the honor to inform you that the Board of Supervisors has granted your request, and furthermore, that it is not the intention of the Chairman of the Board to cut down the tree."

The letter was most revealing. Jim Lewis, chairman of the board of supervisors, was also Hackfeld's contractor! The women's group was pleased but suspicious. The next day, Lewis—the contractor and chairman—asked the Hilo Electric Light Company to remove its light pole, because either the tree or the pole would have to go in order that the building be moved. The utility company said they would move the pole if Hackfeld or the county would guarantee payment of the expense involved. Lewis, speaking for both, refused to pay anything.

Early Saturday morning, three days after the board members assured everyone concerned they would obey the law and not destroy the palm, a crowd gathered in downtown Hilo as Lewis arrived with his crew of workmen and prepared to move the building. Lewis personally addressed a hostile group of women, explaining that he "was not cutting down the tree as prohibited by law, but was bending it over in order that the building might pass over it." The crowd was skeptical and watched apprehensively as Lewis ordered two Hawaiians to climb the palm and secure a rope at the highest point below the splayed fronds. With block and tackle rigged to a horse team, the palm was slowly pulled over. As the top neared the ground, the aged roots, shallow and damaged from traffic in the busy intersection, suddenly cracked loose from the earth. Lewis shrugged his shoulders and ordered the team to continue pulling. The palm jerked free, wrenched from the ground in a cloud of dust, and was dragged to the shore of nearby Hilo Bay to wash out on the tide.

The contractor-chairman disclaimed any violation of law; as he said, the palm was not "cut down." His excuse, that he merely bent it over and that it broke, may help explain the conservationists' continued distrust —more than sixty years later—of developers and politicians, both of whom deny vigorously any conflict of interest.

Over the years conservationists continued to save individual trees from destruction by the same enemy—urban growth. A monkeypod by the courthouse in Wailuku, on Maui, was threatened by a decision to widen the corner so pineapple trucks could turn more easily on their route to the cannery. The tree won. On Kauai, probably the largest *kamani* tree in Hawaii was marked for removal where the new airport access road entered Lihue town. The tree won.

But for every victory there was a defeat, an unnecessary destruction. In Honolulu a traffic engineer ordered removal of a dozen tropical mahogany trees from the Kalakaua Boulevard median strip "to provide turning space for a left turn lane"—a lane that was never used. He showed his concern for the community by cutting the trees without advance notice, starting at 2:00 A.M., to "avoid traffic snarls from public demonstrations."

In 1947, the board of supervisors, this time in Honolulu, voted unanimously to remove a hundred-year-old banyan tree in central Honolulu. Growing at the busy intersection of Keeaumoku and King streets, the banyan's spreading canopy reached across both streets from its position at the intersection and could be seen for blocks in every direction. But its location was both its virtue and its ruin—it was a landmark and a traffic hazard.

The tree may have been one of the first banyans planted in Hawaii. Now it was to be killed to widen a street.

Budget problems intervened. No improvement funds were appropriated that year. The street was not widened and the banyan continued to grow in size and prestige, deflecting increasing traffic from Interstate highway H-1 passing two blocks away and from the giant Ala Moana shopping center between the tree and the ocean.

The supervisors changed to councilmen as the city and county of Honolulu received a new charter, increased population, and new impetus to modernize. In 1963, a vote again was taken to widen the street. Again the banyan lost. During Thanksgiving week the council voted 7 to 2 to chop down the banyan.

The familiar editorials appeared in both daily papers as friends of the banyan joined in the struggle. "Are trees like this to be destroyed because some people are fools, and cannot drive safely without the widest of boulevards?" editorialized the *Honolulu Star Bulletin*. "We do not believe the city will go through with its threat, there are too many people left who respect and revere these already dwindling giants of time and nature that once made Honolulu a park. We believe we are not quite yet gone mad with the idea of turning our city into one vast sea of motor vehicles; and if enough of us protest, and loudly enough, this tree will live."

Students picketed beneath the banyan with placards reading: "Bet you never sat under a highway." As the women of the influential Outdoor Circle prepared for battle, the legislature joined with a resolution supporting the banyan. "In man's mad rush toward the longest, the highest, the widest, there has been a disregard for the aesthetic." The mayor intervened, ordering the tree spared—if at all possible—saying, "if street-widening is undertaken, the banyan will become part of a traffic island."

At this juncture the state joined the skirmish, asserting its rights over the banyan, pointing out that the tree was on state land and that the city and county must obtain its permission before starting the chain saw.

"Well, now, we shall see what we shall see," chortled a *Star Bulletin* editorial. "The City Council says cut down the tree. The Keeaumoku—King Banyan that is. The State says, no sir, can't be done. Tree belongs to the State . . . Sure the city is using the land where the tree is. But the State didn't lend the City the tree, it lent it the land. Tree still belongs to the State."

The city attorney said he was prepared to test in court the city's right to cut down the banyan. The state stood firm, while the land board voted to preserve the tree, and demanded proof that the tree was a traffic hazard. The city council promptly obliged by adopting a resolution, declaring the banyan tree "a traffic hazard that must be eliminated." The document was hand-carried to the state officials.

The first city petition for an improvement district to widen King Street failed when 56 percent of the affected property owners opposed the project—just enough to kill it. The banyan received a temporary reprieve as conservationists marshaled forces for the expected new round of public hearings.

A nearby shopping center offered space for the tree in its parking lot "at no cost." City Hall rejected the idea because the cost of moving the huge tree would be "enormous and prohibitive." The afternoon daily newspaper retained a nurseryman to prepare a "medical report" on the banyan. He said its health was going downhill because the aerial roots were not allowed to grow, but it probably could live another hundred years or more. Proposals to move the tree across the street and farther back into the adjacent park were all turned down as impractical by determined councilmen who could visualize only wide streets as a civic improvement.

The public hearing filled the council chambers. Representatives of every conservation organization in Hawaii, plus numerous individual citizens, pleaded for the banyan's life. An officer of the mainland Federation of Western Outdoor Clubs emotionally testified that "the declaration by a member of the National Council of the Arts that Hawaii is a 'national treasure,' should not be answered by chopping down the prized tree, probably the oldest banyan in Hawaii." "After all," he said, "one-hundred-year-old banyans do not sprout up every day." The council responded by asking for more studies and promised to personally visit the banyan tree. They assured protesters that the city would plant 200 new trees along widened King Street.

When the council finally voted 8 to 1 to kill the tree, conservationists decided the banyan would not die unmourned. The Outdoor Clubs spokesman called for public attendance at the sad event to demonstrate its opposition to "unnecessary destruction of the banyan by the city council . . . we will make it known that this execution of the banyan is not going unnoticed."

Artists arranged for a "paint-in" before Sunday morning, when the tree was finally scheduled for removal by the lowest bidder. Photographers arrived for last pictures, and young students from Punahou locked arms around the tree in a "climb-in" at dawn. Radio KORL set up mobile equipment to broadcast an account of the destruction while the mayor announced plans to perpetuate the now-famous tree by dismembering it and planting its limbs in various parks around the city.

Memorial services were held for the banyan at 7:00 A.M. while the demolition crew quietly stood by. Early Sunday morning traffic slowed to watch. Suddenly the painful whine of chain saws startled the disheartened crowd who stood by to bid farewell. They watched sadly as pieces and parts fell to the street. By Sunday afternoon the doomed tree was gone and the broken branches and fallen leaves raked into convenient piles. Someone erected a small cross in the scarred earth. It remained for several days, reminding the many thousands of drivers passing through the busy intersection that something was missing from Hawaii.

Exactly three months later, Henry Faliu, owner of the local Samoan Tree Trimming Company, received a phone call from someone in the state government asking if his firm would be able to cut down the royal palms around King Kamehameha's statue in front of the Judiciary Building, one of the most significant historical sites in Honolulu's civic center.

Faliu met a state purchasing agent the next morning to work out details. The young *haole* man, dressed neatly in gray coat and colorful tie, showed Faliu the park landscaping plans and explained that so many complaints had been received about the palms that the parks department decided to remove them and plant a low hedge around the famed statue of Kamehameha, the focal point of Hawaiian celebrations during Kamehameha Day.

The agent offered to pay Faliu $225 to remove each palm and uproot the stumps—$1,575 for all seven royal palms. Faliu signed the contract and agreed to begin clearing at six o'clock the next morning and have the job completed before the morning commuter rush. Faliu assigned his Samoan tree trimmers, Siutu Sula and Tolola Malepeai, to the job and an hour after they started work the damage was done.

Early morning traffic came to a halt. First arrivals at the Judiciary Building could not believe their eyes. Older Hawaiians cried. There were tears and clenched fists. Everyone was stunned. But by the time responsible authorities could get on the telephone to stop the desecration, three of the forty-foot-high, eighty-five-year-old royal palms were chopped to the ground and the other four decapitated, their lush palm fronds scattered irreverently about the courthouse lawn.

Reporters searched for answers to the shocking incident as harassed authorities disclaimed responsibility for the outrage. Some-one called it a "vicious practical joke." Chief Justice William Richardson viewed the carnage with somber concern. "I can't imagine a person having so much disregard for beauty," he said, "that he could destroy one of the state's greatest assets." City Councilman Herman Lemke, who had voted to saw down the banyan tree, said, "This is horrible. It'll be a real problem finding replacement trees that match." Dr. Donald Watson, chairman of the University of Hawaii Department of Horticul-ture, voiced a growing sentiment when he said chopping down the trees didn't surprise him at all. "If they'll cut down the banyan tree, they'll do anything."

Someone asked to see the work order—maybe an imposter was involved. Frightened trimmer Faliu, threatened by damage suits and action by irate conservationists, replied that he had no copy; but, he said, the man who authorized him to cut down the trees stated his name was Albert Camus.

THE HILO PALM

While state officials, outraged at the mass murder of the palms, continued to denounce the scheme as a meaningless prank pulled by a "crank . . . a screwball," several members of Honolulu's intellectual community thought they saw a meaningful message in the act. The choice of the name Albert Camus could be no coincidence, they felt, viewed against Hawaii's record of sacrificing historic and aged trees for highways and subdivisions in the name of progress.

Albert Camus—existentialist—writer—philosopher—won the Nobel prize for literature and stressed in his writings man's need to carry out a personal responsibility in the fight against social evil. His themes dwelled on the concept of being and the concept of the absurd, all illuminations on human existence.

One Camus scholar viewed the deliberate tragedy as a symbol of the wrongs we allow to happen in a computerized society. He said, "I think people are missing the whole point if they focus their attention on trying to determine what 'nut' prescribed the royal execution. Rather, the focus should be on why. . . . Maybe, what it all means is that we're all guilty. . . . The most important thing is if the act causes people to ask questions. And in the moment they do, there's hope. A true Camus happening."

Camus, a member of the French Resistance during World War II, wrote, "considered as artists, we perhaps have no need to interfere in the affairs of the world. But considered as men, yes . . . I have written so much, and perhaps too much, only because I cannot keep from being drawn toward everyday life, toward those, whoever they may be, who are humiliated and debased. It seems to me impossible to endure that idea, nor can he who cannot endure it lie down to sleep in his tower."

The royal palms were never replaced.

Maui

Valley Island

Haleakala—House of the Sun. In Hawaiian legend and Polynesian lore, the demigod Maui snared the Sun God above Haleakala on his daily path across the mountain, forcing him to slow his flight and provide more time to fish and repair nets. Koolau Gap breaks the crater wall where ancient lava overflowed down Keanae Valley to the sea.

ALONG THE LONG, winding road east out of Paia, past the orderly taro fields of Keanae and Wailua, beyond the old rubber plantation at Nahiku, and past Waianapanapa, where the early evening rain rattles the pandanus leaves, lives the largest single community of Hawaiian people—descendants of the bold seafarers who sailed their double-hulled canoes thousands of trackless miles north from Tahiti and Samoa to a new world.

The last Hawaiians live on a rural landscape, emulating as best they can, in a modern world, the life-style of a hundred years past. The men are cowboys instead of warriors; but their women, huge in the manner of King Kamehameha's favorite Hana queen, still *hānai* their babies, in which all the community shares in raising all the children. No child is without a family in the Hawaiian world.

The famous Hana road, winding fifty miles and a hundred curves from Paia to Kaupo, is one of America's great scenic drives. Unique in terms of semitropical landscape and absence of urban blight, the road is endorsed by Friends of the Earth for designation as Maui National Parkway to preserve its exotic visual beauty exactly as it is. There is no way to improve this exciting road; to straighten the curves is to destroy it. It is a destination in itself. Visitors in a hurry to reach Hana fly—the short way.

Maui's rural Hana district is a sea-level *lānai* (front porch) for Haleakala, the 10,023-foot-high extinct volcano dominating East Maui

and Haleakala National Park. Its cinder-pocketed crater is twenty-one miles in circumference, enclosing one of only two nesting areas for Hawaii's state bird, the rare nene goose. Only about 200 birds survive. Higher in the crater unusual silversword plants bloom in August, sending up a plume of several hundred blossoms on a six- to eight-foot stalk. After growing slowly like silver-spiked balls for a decade or more, the silversword blooms once, then dies.

Along the eastern rim a new extension of the park (donated by the Nature Conservancy, the state of Hawaii, and ranch-owner Jean McCaughey) connects the summit to the sea at Seven Pools. The wild Kipahulu Valley, home of endangered birds found nowhere else in Hawaii, is maintained within the park as a wilderness preserve.

Haleakala and East Maui are the wild, scenic Maui, contrasting with the loud, tourist-oriented West Maui, known mostly for its Iao Needle (in reality a narrow ridge), and the elaborate resorts at Kaanapali, which are flanked by a plaque of speculator-owned condominium apartments disrupting the ocean view at every turn in the road beyond Lahaina. They are ugly blemishes on the gentle Hawaiian landscape, for little aesthetic concern exists among the mélange of investors who barter the scenic beauty of West Maui for profit.

Amfac's private resort preserve of Kaanapali offers the excitement and night life of an urban center in a setting of dramatic beauty. The warm sun sets in full glowing drama behind the gentle profile of Lanai Island nine miles across the channel. To the south is Kahoolawe Island, to the north Molokai. It is an island world floating on calm seas, once host in whaling days to a hundred and more Boston ships at a time, waiting out the Arctic winter in a sheltered anchorage. In season whales still cavort offshore, their spouting a signal for local whale watchers from Honolulu to join the tourists at Kaanapali bars.

The morning sun is fortunately late in rising at Kaanapali: it must clear the precipitous West Maui mountains sweeping dramatically upward to cloud-shrouded peaks behind Lahaina. They are a grand backdrop to the green carpet of sugar and symmetric patterns of pineapple fields fringing the Royal Lahaina Golf Club's close-cropped greens and sand traps. Kaanapali plays well on nature's island stage, man's agriculture and games blending into a drama of green and blue. Kaanapali must be one of only a few large resort complexes—the only one in Hawaii—that seriously attempts to preserve scenic amenities while offering high-rise resort excitement. Design controls and sign regulations on leased hotel

sites are tighter than state and county government restrictions. No flashing neon exists in Kaanapali. In the entire state of Hawaii only nearby Lahaina says "be careful" with greater emphasis.

Lahaina is the only zoned historical district in Hawaii and offers a whaling port sampling combined with the missionary outpost of a hundred years ago. Early trading stores established by sea captains occupied spaces that are now filled with tourist gift shops and exotic restaurants. One café is perched in a tree; another is in a second-story loft without walls, atop one of the first buildings in Lahaina.

The seventy-one-year-old Pioneer inn still services customers with baths down the hall, a tilting grand staircase, and the same bar rail that was shipped around the Horn. Newer rooms are available for those who are less nostalgic; but the cook-your-own-steak outdoor dining room captures a dated world atmosphere unique to Maui.

Where highway pavement ends, most Maui roads continue as rough, narrow lanes between *koa-haole* brush and across rock-strewn fields, sometimes going up and down, but usually back and forth. Constructed mostly by prison labor, these roads circle the island completely, giving only Maui the distinction of true round-the-island exploration by conventional sedan.

The Polynesians created their own version of the Roman god Hercules. They called him "Maui" and ascribed to him amazing feats of creation. It was the demigod Maui who helped arrange the Hawaiian Islands as they are today. He raised the sky so man could walk standing up. His name is used by ocean people from New Zealand to Hawaii as an oath to scare misbehaving children.

Maui Island was the scene of his greatest exploit. Wielding a net woven from the pubic hair of his sister, Maui lassoed the Sun God between the legs and slowed his daily flight around the earth. Beating the sun with his grandmother's jawbone, Maui convinced the fast-moving god to slow his travel across the sky and provide more daylight for men to fish and mend their nets. Maui gave the world a full day.

SEVEN POOLS, HALEAKALA NATIONAL PARK

EARLY MORNING WIND, KEANAE

124 MAUI

Deep, tangled forests of Hawaiian hardwood trees are the tropical counterpoint to slender Iao Needle standing vertically against the steep walls of Iao Valley. Remnant of an ancient volcanic cone, the famed needle entices many reckless climbers to try their skill. Few have made it to the top. The climb is discouraged by private owners. No trees cling to the treacherous slopes, contrasting with the rain forest jungle of Kipahulu Valley where indigenous 'ōhi'a-lehua trees shelter scarce birds found nowhere else on earth. Kipahulu Valley became part of Haleakala National Park in 1972 when private donors and the state of Hawaii deeded 3,690 acres to the Department of the Interior.

Haleakala Crater is the eroded caldera of a dormant volcano that last erupted on its outer slopes well over a hundred years ago. The aging mountain produced symmetrical cinder cones in a last eruptive gasp of the dying volcano, now host for rare silversword plants speckling the crater floor. The silversword grows slowly for a dozen years, then suddenly raises multiflowered stalks six feet high to blossom only once, then die. Haleakala has always been a sacred place to Hawaiians on the well-traveled trail across the island from Kaupo to Kahului. The umbilical cords of Kaupo babies were often dropped into the "bottomless pit" at the crater's center in a belief that respectful disposition of the cords made children strong. Here also was a sacred spatter cone where the mere disturbance of a single pebble would bring fog, rain, and possible death.

West Maui is where the people are. The county seat at Wailuku, nestled against the West Maui mountains at the entrance to Iao Valley, is the oldest of Maui's "twin" cities. With its neighbor, the port and commercial center, Kahului, it shares a common boundary in the sand dunes above Kahului Bay, where the highways split to circle the island. The Pioneer sugar mill processes cane grown on the island's west shore, where green fields of sugarcane protect the Kaanapali environment from spreading subdivisions. Afternoon clouds cling to the upper slopes where evening rains overflow the mountaintop swamps, bringing water to the dry leeward side.

SUGARCANE TASSELS

From Honolulu International Airport to Maui Island is only twenty-eight minutes by Aloha Airlines Boeing 737, but the time span in life-styles is many hundreds of years. Irrigated taro patches on rural Keanae peninsula were under cultivation when Capt. James Cook anchored offshore in 1778 and first met ruling chief Kalaniopuu and the young warrior Kamehameha, who would later become the first king of Hawaii.

The demigod Maui—a Hercules of Polynesian mythology—placed the Hawaiian Islands where they are today after he caused them to break loose while they were being towed across the ocean. They eventually were left over hot spots on the ocean floor, floating like Maui Island, in the clouds and upon the sea as Polynesians sighted them centuries ago.

The Women Buy the Billboards

SIXTY YEARS AGO a garish wall of billboards blocked the view of Honolulu from Waialae Road. Ten-foot-high letters on the high slopes of Punchbowl touted the merits of soap. Along the streetcar line to Waikiki, Diamond Head was hidden behind billboards that hawked catsup, tamales, and whiskey. Green pickles were featured on the Nuuanu Pali road crossing to windward Oahu.

The Pioneer Advertising Company held the monopoly on Honolulu billboard advertising, and their forty clients were effectively blotting out choice portions of the Hawaiian landscape. Prime view areas in Honolulu were already tacky with garish signs, some embellished with Victorian trim. Local distributors and mainland manufacturers were busy with designs for more, and the best scenic sites were out for bids.

In 1913 a determined group of white women, all wives of influential local businessmen, decided to eliminate outdoor advertising in Hawaii. When the exclusive Kilohana Art League was disbanded, they established the Outdoor Circle Committee as an independent women's club to promote civic betterment, specifically "to rid the city of billboards." They started with thirty members and plenty of enthusiasm.

Their first president offered to buy the billboard company; but when members learned that the asking price was ten times their meager resources, war clouds gathered and the women decided on an organized boycott of all outdoor advertisers. The firms were notified accordingly and reminded tactfully that the upper-class Outdoor Circle members made substantial household purchases. It was a convincing argument.

A rubber stamp was used to mark every check, bill, and letterhead with two-inch-high red letters identifying the sender as "ANTI BILLBOARD." When new billboards advertising a popular baking powder appeared along the street one morning, the local distributor received an avalanche of personal letters explaining that as long as the baking powder remained on the billboards in Hawaii ". . . we will be forced to find another brand to use and recommend to our friends and acquaintances." The women of the Outdoor Circle shortly received a cable saying the firm had canceled its outdoor advertising contract and would immediately remove the offending advertisements.

It was a time when a woman's place was definitely in the home, and staid Honolulu businessmen were not quite prepared to cope effectively with women as adversaries meddling in their affairs. They could hardly guess that this group of middle-aged matrons in high-necked shirtwaists, hobble skirts, and *lau hala* hats would make billboards both unpopular and unprofitable within a few years.

The women directly challenged downtown merchants and asked for and received the endorsement of their cause by the Honolulu Chamber of Commerce. One of the Honolulu daily newspapers published a special edition, edited by the campaigning women, that featured a front page photograph of billboards captioned, "Once the Finest View on Waialae Road." The fledgling Hawaiian tourist bureau unanimously endorsed the ladies' campaign at a time when preserving scenic beauty was mostly an idea and when getting involved was to be avoided. The Honolulu Board of Supervisors voted its appreciation and support.

In four years the number of billboard advertisers steadily dropped from forty to six. The boycott was clearly effective, yet several large—twenty-four-sheet—poster boards still cluttered the streets.

The remaining advertisers were simply given more space. Meanwhile, in an attempt to placate the ladies of the Outdoor Circle, decorative boards were put up in new sites. The women refused to compromise, holding out for total capitulation; but years passed without surrender.

In 1927 only Wrigley's chewing gum and national cigarette advertisements remained on the boards. Increased antagonism of the community against outdoor advertising had long since discouraged local firms from promoting their products outdoors. The Outdoor Circle tried again to buy the billboards and this time found a defeated company only too willing. There was little business left and the price was cheap. The Outdoor Circle raised $4,000 among their members and became—for one week—the only citizen conservation organization in the outdoor advertising business. It took them that long to cancel the remaining contracts, dismantle the signboards, and burn the termite-infested remains in a funeral pyre. Diamond Head could be seen again from the Waikiki streetcar.

During the hot summer days of 1927, Hawaii's territorial governor signed into law a bill passed by the Republican legislature effectively banning all outdoor advertising in Hawaii. Subsequent amendments over the years allowed only point of sale and business identification signs, which were limited in size by county ordinances.

Now even temporary political posters are prohibited. Name stickers on trees and poles are outlawed—they are legally classified as litter. Only the bumper sticker and lapel button remain unregulated in Hawaii.

Barbed wire restricted the use of Waikiki Beach during World War II. Beyond Punchbowl National Memorial Cemetery of the Pacific is Diamond Head.

Ua mau ke ea o ka ʻāina i ka pono

"The life of the land is perpetuated in righteousness."
Motto of the kingdom and the state of Hawaii.

IN A TIME when ethnic minorities are fighting in defense of racial integrity and self-determination, the question is often asked why the native Hawaiian people failed to seriously challenge the take-over of their islands by American sugar planters and traders.

Feeble resistance by supporters of the last Hawaiian queen, Liliuokalani, composer of *Aloha ʻOe,* only emphasized the general apathy of Hawaiians as a racial group, who willingly accepted the virtual extermination of their cultural traditions by missionaries, who suffered widespread decimation of the race by Western disease—bubonic plague and smallpox, measles and syphilis—and who lost their land to Western concepts of economic democracy and private property.

Following annexation of the islands as a United States territory, white planters and traders supported the Hawaiian delegate to the United States Congress, Prince Jonah Kuhio, in his plea for Hawaiian homesteading land. This gesture apparently resulted from the adverse criticism of their ruthless take-over of the sovereign Hawaiian kingdom. Congress authorized the establishment of a reservation system, ostensibly offering the Hawaiians an opportunity to return to the land. The only requirement was that they farm it and live on it.

Unfortunately, after American businessmen and the military took the choicest parcels, most of the land remaining for the Hawaiians was marginal at best, little suited to small-farm agriculture, and without water or access. After numerous farms had failed, it became clear also that few Hawaiians really enjoyed the hard work of farming. They found easy loopholes in the agreements and subleased the land to pineapple growers and ranchers, who paid them a nominal rental.

In time, many homestead areas, particularly in Honolulu, deteriorated into rural slums when traditional Hawaiian family relationships broke down in the clash with competitive urban demands generated by a money economy. The adults too often were on welfare, and their children delinquent. Families desiring credit for a new car or color TV were frustrated by a high cost of living requiring that both mother and father work in expensive Hawaii, further worsening traditional family relationships. In some cases the artificial security of a free homestead seemed to smother the Hawaiian spirit.

Opportunities for Hawaiians in skilled employment were scarce, and what success they did achieve appeared to them to be racial tokenism rather than a proud contribution to society. Too often the hotel-room maid, the bellboy, and the janitor were Hawaiians. There were more dropouts than graduates from high school, and the police lineup seemed to increasingly repeat Hawaiian surnames. It was only a matter of time before young part-Hawaiians became radicalized, and they identified the increasing urbanization of Hawaii and the accompanying depreciation of rural lifestyles as the social culprits.

Disrespect for the land allowed speculators to run bulldozers across agricultural fields with little opposition, until the rising prices of land and housing crowded all but the most affluent off the land. Because Honolulu was identified by federal agencies as the second most expensive city in the world in terms of daily living costs, it became evident that perhaps a closer concern for land use was needed: perhaps unrestricted growth and subdivision of the land of Hawaii were mistakes.

Environmentalists have a word for the close relationship between people and the land—between nature and all other living things. It's called ecology. And when Hawaii is thought of as a closed island ecosystem, the folly of continued urbanization becomes self-evident. Not only is the future economic solvency of sugar and pineapple jeopardized, but so are the scenic assets of a valuable tourist industry. Even more, it is rapidly becoming too expensive for the people who work in Hawaii to live in Hawaii.

The state itself took the first step to help preserve agricultural lands by withdrawing all primary zoning rights from county governments and initiating land-use zoning by the state for all lands, public and private. It helped reduce the destructive "chamber of commerce" competition between the counties and made difficult the acquisition of favorable zoning decisions by private developers—the state being more difficult to corrupt than the counties.

As an aroused community gradually resisted encroachment of sprawling subdivisions upon agricultural land and expansion of hotel facilities into scenic and historical areas, battles were won and lost in the state and county political arenas. However, even the losses were gains in some ways. Every loss saw a newly irate community or social group decrying the irresponsible builders and "developer oriented" legislators. The matter of saving the land became a political issue. The mayor of Honolulu won a close election, in large part, with his commitment to "save Diamond Head."

The basic issue of stockholder interests versus people became relevant when the Kohala Sugar Company announced it would shut down because the company was no longer earning sufficient profits. Suddenly everything became clearer—the use of the land was better understood. The sugar workers' union and the county governments demanded that Kohala continue in operation. The county recommended buying the company and having the people of Hawaii grow the sugar, but the state legislature refused to appropriate the money.

Seemingly unrelated events created headlines. On Oahu, pig farmers in Kalama Valley were joined by young counterculture people in opposing the elimination of small farms and house lots at Henry Kaiser's Hawaii Kai project, which were to be replaced by expensive residential subdivisions. They lost, after staging a sit-in before the bulldozer. The police dragged them away as they were pleading for the right to live on the land Hawaiian Princess Bernice Pauahi Bishop inherited from their ancestors and leased to Kaiser.

When the state of Hawaii completed the purchase of Kahana Valley on Oahu's windward shore to create a great state park, authorities immediately issued eviction notices requiring the Hawaiian residents to move from the valley. They refused, and the resulting outcry forced the division of state parks to reevaluate its construction plans: perhaps it would be appropriate after all, they said, for Hawaiians to live in a park on their land.

Kahana residents wanted to take part in this new concept—a "living park"—and were supported by the governor's task force for Kahana Valley. A bill was introduced in the legislature, determining that "if the Land Department finds . . . that the original residents of the park area enhance the land or have a culturally or historically valuable lifestyle, these residents shall be allowed to remain on the state park lands." It would have been a great cultural step forward for Hawaii to officially recognize the Hawaiians' plea, but the bill failed to pass. But neither was any further move made by the state to evict the 140 residents of Kahana Valley.

The spokesman for the valley Hawaiians, Lydia Dela Cerra, whose mixed racial parentage is revealed in her name, said, "This valley has housed our ancestors for many, many years. Isn't it a privilege that we, the offspring of Hawaiian ancestry, should be given rights to remain in the valley which once held the Hawaiiana [traditions] of the natives here, which is slowly dispersing into thin air?"

A new pattern was appearing in the valley dwellers' plea, one that echoed a different cry than that of conventional environmentalist objections to expanding highways and sprawling subdivisions. The Hawaiians were presenting a petition to the private estates and public land administrators stating that the land they lived on was theirs by right of birth, that no one owns the land, that "the land is ours to hold in trust for our children and generations to come." Suddenly the controversy developed into a political challenge of the basic concepts of private property and the laws perpetuating the giant land trusts.

The current struggle may have begun in the mid-1960s, when newly elected Gov. John Burns appointed a militant conservationist to the state Land Use Commission. The conservationist and the governor's director of planning and economic development joined in opposing urban zoning of Oahu's south shore beyond Sandy Beach. When the Hawaii Kai development people learned of this opposition to their plans, Henry Kaiser himself drove downtown to the Land Use Commission office and, with his associates waiting hesitantly in the hallways, loudly expressed his extreme displeasure at a public zoning body that would

deny him the right to do anything he wanted with his land. Kaiser said he would sue and threatened to abandon the entire multimillion-dollar Kaiser Hawaii Kai project unless he immediately received permission to build hotels on Sandy Beach and homes on every ridge. The "progress and growth" oriented commission retreated quickly, and the final vote granted Kaiser almost everything he demanded. The small farmers and Hawaiian families living deep inside Kalama Valley were never consulted. No public hearing notice was posted along the dirt roads leading inland among the dry windblown *kiawe* trees bordering Sandy Beach. The zoning change was decided by Kaiser and the state only.

The hopes of Kalama Valley farmers and squatters, enjoying a semisubsistence lifestyle, were briefly revived when a bill was introduced in the 1971 legislature suggesting that the rural life in southern Oahu should not

completely disappear. Senator Nadao Yoshinaga charged that "the proposed urban development of Kalama Valley is an example of mismanagement and misuse by the land owner, a charitable trust, and is a threat to the welfare of the State."

The senator in his bill called for a study of population stabilization in a racially and economically mixed community, which would include former residents of the valley who were forced out to make room for the Kaiser subdivision. He also asked for a planned land development program that would include open spaces, recreational, agricultural, and conservation areas, as well as individually styled communities appropriate to counterculture lifestyles of people who want to live on the land in their own way in hand-built structures exempt from conventional building codes. Education for children and adults would be integrated into community life and include

TARO PATCHES, HALAWA VALLEY, MOLOKAI

HAMOA SHORE, MAUI

MILOLII VILLAGE, HAWAII

participation in civic, artistic, and cultural affairs.

The bill was defeated by a legislative majority that would have none of this rural life-style nonsense.

In the spring of 1972, a disenchanted group of young people met again at Henry Kaiser's development near Sandy Beach to offer a requiem for the last open shoreline of the Bishop Estate on southern Oahu Island—a shoreline being bulldozed for development into a modern resort-hotel complex. The evicted farmers were there, along with the young part-Hawaiians and friends of every racial mix, dancing to a rock beat, asking in plaintive song why only the rich could live in Hawaii.

On the Big Island, ten organizations joined together to oppose construction of public golf courses and a realigned highway near Keala-kekua Bay, where Captain Cook first landed. They called for a public hearing and complained that the newly appointed Bishop Estate trustee, Matsuo Takabuki, had "never discussed any of these plans with us. Takabuki should come to this public hearing and find out what the Hawaiian people want."

Concern was expressed for the Hawaiians who lived on small land parcels along the isolated Napoopoo shore. They claimed that the Bishop Estate planned a community of 8,800 persons with 88 acres of hotels and that the crowds of people would "force us off our land, deny us our beaches, and pollute our fishing waters." Their spokesman said zoning would not protect the Hawaiians, because "the tax collector will take away everything when the rich mainlanders move in."

Hawaiians living in the great Kahaluu bowl along Oahu's upper Kaneohe Bay joined the cultural rebellion, forming their own community association to oppose irresponsible government-sponsored development and to protect traditional rural life-styles against the onslaught of urban subdividers steadily advancing north from Honolulu.

"We love our land," said Lucy Naluai, the quiet chairman of Hui Mālama 'Aina Ko'olau, a community organization whose goals include the "protection and loving care of our kuleana," the personal property handed down through generations after the great division of land among the commoners and the chiefs by King Kamehameha III.

"We also love our ancestors," said Lucy Naluai, "and we cannot and will not see them ripped out of the land by bulldozers. They kill a little bit of us every time they take our land."

Some of the people evicted from Kaiser's development moved to Kahaluu, where, according to Hui Mālama spokesmen, they are "broken people, many of them forced to live on welfare because their sources of income were destroyed and their rents went up. . . . Now, there are no more Kahaluus that they can go to."

The demands of Hui Mālama are simple —stop all capital improvement projects financed by public funds that would accelerate population growth and increase land costs and taxes. They criticize the planned Interstate H-3 freeway crossing the island, which "will allow many people . . . from Honolulu to move to Kahaluu and make Kahaluu into a rich suburb. There will be a lot of expensive housing development which we cannot afford." "It must not be built," they say.

The proposed Kahaluu flood-control project "will make commercial, resort, and industrial development possible . . . [and] further drive up the cost of the land," according to Hui Mālama. "If the land is not cleared and bulldozed there will be no floods to bother us," so a flood-control project would not be necessary.

Regarding the harbor proposed by the United States Corps of Engineers to accommodate 1,600 small boats, the Hawaiians conjecture that "the only reason we can think of for [this] project is that someone wants to attract rich people to move over here. . . . We don't need it." And they add, "the new sewage treatment plant will not be needed if no more people move out here, and if the highway isn't

PUNA, HAWAII

built the people won't come. . . . The treatment plant would only facilitate tourism activities and wealthy residential construction.''

The Hawaiians, born of the islands and custodians of the rich culture and traditions of a Polynesian civilization, see their language and unique life-style disappearing. With perhaps less than 8,000 pureblooded Hawaiians remaining, they see the entire race nearing extinction. They do not pretend they can stop development, but they do ask to participate in the decisions that shape their future and their land.

''We demand that it be development that builds on the life of the people,'' says *Hui Mālama,* ''that preserves our values, and that nourishes the children and grandchildren of all the native people of Hawaii. We cannot any more allow development that destroys the things that make Hawaii what it is.''

Hawaii Tomorrow

HAWAII STILL MAINTAINS aspects of traditional life-styles which our immigrant parents and grandparents brought with them from overseas. Our Polynesian ties are also strong, and those of us from other parts of the world have been stimulated by the spirit of the native Hawaiians who came here long before everyone else. At the same time we are Americans living in the fiftieth state of the Union. All of these people have combined to give birth to what can be called an "island life-style"—a blending of many life-styles into a social order which respects differences and which is based on a unique island environment.

Over the past few decades there have been many changes in the islands. Some of these have been very beneficial while others have been less so. The effects of many of these changes have been harmful to the environment. For the most part, these changes can be attributed to growth. Growth has occurred in many ways and has been exciting and challenging; it has also brought about problems and unforeseen consequences. Growth in our population, our economy, and our standard of living has created a somewhat lesser environment for our people. Although the people of Hawaii enjoy a quality of environment that other areas of the world have long since lost, we are realizing that both preventive and corrective measures are urgently needed to maintain that quality and to protect our national beauty.

Serious attempts are being made to assure the protection of our natural resources and the preservation of the natural beauty of the islands which have been enjoyed for generations. The impact of the visitor industry is being carefully scrutinized, as is urbanization and all other forms of development. Outside of Waikiki, resort facilities have been created in essentially rural areas, and the social and environmental impact of such developments has been great. Scattered and sprawling urbanization has also taken over some of our prime agricultural lands, yet agriculture, in addition to providing the basis of our economy, has contributed to keeping the landscape in open space.

Islands are basically closed systems in the sense that change in one aspect of the system, even if it is a small one, will have effects on the rest of the system. The space limitation of an island magnifies changes, making even relatively small changes capable of rather profound general effects. Any growth which occurs in this fragile system must be accommodated while maintaining environmental quality.

As our population increases, the desire to experience natural beauty and the need to protect our natural resources will grow. The number of competing uses for various lands will likewise increase, and if uncontrolled, the development necessary to accommodate an increasing population will have detrimental effects on our natural resources and beauty—gifts of nature that are irreplaceable assets of public trust.

Hawaii has progressed to a stage of sincere self-scrutiny. For the physical, social, and psychological well-being of our residents it is necessary that there be a continuation of those aspects of our environment and our lives which we deem valuable. Expressions of concern have been heard about the loss of the island way of life. The island life-style cannot be separated from the island environment, and concern over the degra-dation of our environment has also been expressed. These concerns are continually growing. We strongly feel that Hawaii is special, and that planning efforts should attempt to retain the beauty of the islands, to provide for orderly growth without destroying our natural and cultural resources, and to make Hawaii a healthy place in which to live and to visit.

Various concepts for protecting our agricultural lands are being supported by our legislators. For a decade Hawaii has had a state law designed expressly to protect prime agricultural lands, forest lands, and scenic areas from urban encroachment. Other concepts now being considered include land banks, agricultural preserves, and greater tax incentives. The basis for protecting agricultural lands is not merely economic, but social and physical as well. The desire to continue a life-style based on agriculture has been strongly expressed, and we must provide the opportunity for our agricultural community to continue.

Although it has been partially accomplished, it is necessary that we further determine the carrying capacity of our land for various and appropriate uses. In doing this, long-range decisions would be based on what the land can handle, with the amount of environmental degradation kept at a minimum.

Establishment of an optimum population for Hawaii is inevitable. As people realize the environmental and social degradation associated with continued population growth *ad infinitum,* the natural growth rate will stabilize. In-migration to Hawaii will also stabilize as work opportunities come into balance and the visitor industry more carefully prices its product to attract a quality clientele. If we understand the carrying capacity of our land, we will be better able to cope with growth and determine to what extent orderly development can be accommodated in years to come.

Hawaii is becoming an increasingly popular tourist area. Lower air fares and appropriately priced accommodations enable more people to visit the islands. The industry itself has made great efforts to attract visitors from throughout the world. Hawaii has enjoyed the fruits of the industry. However, we have become aware of the less positive economic, social, and environmental impact of the visitor industry. In order to improve the quality of the services offered to the visitor, and to better realize the benefits of the industry, there is a need to carefully examine the growth of the industry. For example, efforts should be spent on establishing specific and concentrated visitor destination areas that would not encroach upon open space and scenic vistas. Such areas would be determined by the carrying capacity of the land, the weighing of alternative uses of the land in relation to public recreation opportunities and natural resources, and, very importantly, the effect of development on the life-style of the resident population—the people who live in Hawaii.

Future economic endeavors will have to be more fully compatible with social and environmental desires. Growth in any form should not be detrimental to our well-being. Hawaii will surely be able to prosper in the future as a beautiful chain of islands, a true home for its residents, with a dynamic island life-style, and a total experience for the visitors to be shared and carried home within their hearts.

Mayor SHUNICHI KIMURA
County of Hawaii

Hawaii

PETROGLYPH NEAR KALAPANA

Most of the tiny church structures built in picturesque communities around the island are legacies of active missionary times, when every village boasted of its own church and congregation. The villages have long since disappeared, but their churches, like Kahaluu in North Kona, remain as quiet refuges for passing visitors.

HAWAII, LARGEST OF the Hawaiian Islands and one of the newest islands in the Pacific, was born only a little over one million years ago on a molten upwelling of magma from the ocean floor. Hawaii Island is still growing, its volcanic vents among the world's most active. Lava still flowed into the sea in 1971 near Kalapana. In 1960 lava flows set afire and then buried the tiny village of Kapoho in Puna, pouring into the sea toward California at Cape Kumukahi.

Ownership of the new Kapoho land is still undecided, although first judgments favored the state, when they claimed traditional accretion rights. Richard Lyman, trustee of Hawaii's giant Bishop Estate and owner of the new volcano, said during the eruption that it must be his land since the volcanic rift opened up on his property—the lava was therefore his lava. One local humorist suggested that, at the very least, since Hawaii was now closer to California by 600 feet, islanders should ask for a reduction in air fare.

Measuring over 30,000 feet from its base on the ocean floor, Hawaii's extinct Mauna Kea is the highest mountain on earth—higher than Everest. Snowcapped every winter with its sister, Mauna Loa, the twin mountains rise over 13,600 feet above sea level and present a spectacular backdrop for Hilo town, spread thinly around crescent-shaped Hilo Bay. Local snow enthusiasts ski in winter while tourist sun worshipers lounge around the palm-shaded Naniloa Hotel pool. From tropical poolside to

mountain summit is only three hours by four-wheel-drive vehicle.

All day, rain will saturate the windward Hamakua Coast while to leeward, Kona residents bask in a warm sun. Hilo molds under an annual rainfall averaging 140 inches while Kawaihae across the island dries out with about 20—generally falling all at once. Greater differences exist between the daily weather in the east and west sides than between summer and winter. When it is raining in the morning there will still be someplace around the island for a dry picnic.

Hawaii escapes hurricane winds from the southwestern Pacific, yet lies far enough north to enjoy westward blowing trade winds while sharing the low sun of southern latitudes. Travel from sea level to higher elevations offers a wide range of temperature, allowing informal dress and living to reflect weather never too hot nor too cold. The weather that changes from side to side and up and down is best enjoyed in Kona, where coffee grows in the shade cast by clouds spreading out from cold 8,251-foot Mount Hualalai every afternoon. A light rain follows, steaming the belt road, gently drifting *makai* (toward the sea) over the honky-tonk resort community spotted in narrow strips along the shore between Kailua and Keauhou. Mountain rains cool the humid afternoon, on schedule, to meet late-arriving tour buses.

Over 90,000 subdivided lots checkerboard the island landscape—few improved with homes—most of them inaccessible over unpaved private roads slowly returning to the jungle. Spawned by speculative developers and mainland corporations, the many thousands of empty parcels represent a risky land investment for visitors yearning to share Hawaii's skyrocketing property values.

Subdivided lots covering parched grasslands of South Kohala and South Point are arid and windswept—unpleasant most of the year—impossible for traditional Hawaiian outdoor living. Parcels in Puna and South Kona, sold to Californians by suedeshoe salesmen passing out bold, colorful brochures describing a South Pacific paradise, are perched atop active volcanic rift zones. The land is subject to destruction by rampaging lava flows at any moment. Every year thousands of disillusioned investors default on monthly payments covering incredible hidden interest balloons. Others default on tax bills reflecting assessments on "wasteland." Auctions by state tax commissioners offer bargains that are quickly bid for resale by unscrupulous salesmen waiting for the latest escapees from California smog who are looking for their dream home in Hawaii.

Their disappointment is expensive.

Hilo, county seat of Hawaii County, second-largest city in the state, is the home of 26,353 residents threatened from both sides by disaster. At any time a *tsunami* (tidal wave) generated by earthquakes in Chile or Alaska may sweep inland from Hilo Bay and engulf coastal dwellings. Volcanologists have yet to predict sudden ruptures in the earth's crust that at any moment may send down from the mountains a destructive lava flow to cover Hilo.

It would be difficult to find a Hilo resident actually worried over these two reminders of doom. The high mountain slopes and quiet sea, deep blue to the distant horizon, hide well the violent vagaries of nature.

The Hilo Yacht Club has no boats, but its trim clubhouse and pool—rebuilt from scratch after the 1946 *tsunami*—is still the gathering place for Hilo's white elite, carefully hanging on to an exclusive remnant of old plantation days. The tourist is welcomed as a guest, but new Hilo residents find breaking into Hilo society a long, arduous task. Between clannish Hilo and stuffy Waimea, the upper class still reigns in a sugar and cattle nostalgia.

Improved federal aid highways connect Waimea to Hilo along the "Scotch Coast," the old domain of imported Scotch sugar plantation managers, their isolated children still speaking with a distant brogue. Old-timers visiting unsuspecting mainland friends "speak Hawaiian" by reciting the names of Hamakua Coast towns with appropriate syllabic accent: Papaikou-Onomea-Pepeekeo-Honomu-Hakalau-Honohina-Ninole-Papaaloa-Laupahoehoe-Ookala-Kukaiau-Paauilo-Paauhau-Honokaa! The demonstration is impressively accomplished in a single breath.

Southward from Hilo, the Volcano Road climbs steadily up Mauna Loa's gentle slope built up from thin lava flows spewed out over thousands of years. The yearly rainfall, averaging 140 inches, has created a vast jungle of indigenous *'ōhi'a-lehua* trees and giant *hāpu'u* ferns blanketing hundreds of square miles that lie above the lowland sugar fields. Within the boundaries of Hawaii Volcanoes National Park, the giant fern forest reaches heights of fifteen feet and more in the seemingly perpetual mist shrouding active Kilauea volcano.

Early American traders soon discovered that *pulu,* the soft fuzz growing at the base of fern stalks, earned a good price in Asia. Chinese purchased the fluffy down by the bale to stuff pillows and mattresses. Fragrant sandalwood growing in the same forest was sold extensively for silk-kimono chests and furniture. Hawaiian chiefs stripped their mountainlands down to the last stick of sandalwood to satisfy the Chinese market. Fern recovered, but the sandalwood did not. Rare sandalwood speci-

mens growing on national park nature trails are not identified. Tourist souvenir hunters would emulate the chiefs and uproot the last tree—if they could find it.

Volcanoes are gentle in Hawaii. Residents rush to view them when word of a new eruption spreads. As the earth splits open with the first hot spurts of orange magma, the news displaces all else on radio networks. Within minutes aircraft are overhead and parking lots fill while the "drive-in" volcanoes display their awesome cauldron of 2,000-degree molten rock to visitors from across the island and around the world. Volcanologists virtually camp on the crater rim to measure the daily gasps and upheavals of mother earth. Occasionally Kilauea puts on a spectacular show, fountaining up as high as 1,900 feet or pumping out lava rivers reaching speeds of thirty knots in a swift dash to the sea. Only then do visitors move back.

Mauna Loa's huge lava mass hides its 13,680-foot height within sloping flanks so gradual that hikers on the summit cannot see over the side to the island below. A distant horizon is their only view. Mauna Loa's high Mokuaweoweo crater last erupted in 1942, and news was censored from the local press because knowledge of the glowing volcano might offer a directional beacon to enemy warships.

Hawaii County's Civil Defense unit called for an immediate evacuation when harmonic tremors indicating movement of molten magma beneath the surface were recorded on portable seismographs. The flank outbreak of Kilauea volcano split open the earth a day later in the orchid fields and papaya groves of Kapoho village. A curtain of fire a mile long erupted from the earth, and lava spread across the land. Groundwater entering superheated vents surfaced amid billowing clouds of steam and continuous explosions raining a storm of cinders and debris on the carefully tended farms. The roar was heard twenty miles away. Lava poured from the vent—molten rock at 1,700 degrees flowed into the sea, covered roads and forests, and overwhelmed earthen dikes hastily bulldozed to protect Kapoho. The small Puna community was set ablaze by the heat of advancing lava and buried beneath forty feet of molten rock.

In 1941 a rampaging Mauna Loa flow was bombed by United States Air Force planes a few miles uphill from Hilo to disperse the threatening lava. Lava fountains stopped the next day, and the creeping *aa* flow cooled to a halt—naturally.

Apollo astronauts visited Kilauea's volcanic landscape in preparation for their first voyages to the moon. It turned out to be an excellent preview for them—the actual moonscape being only more dusty and gray instead of black.

The southwest rift of Kilauea, a separate volcano perched on the side of Mauna Loa, justifies its name in a ten-mile crack stretching across the Kau desert. Beyond, at South Point, is the southern rift of Mauna Loa—the southernmost land in the United States, where early Polynesian voyagers exploring the unknown Pacific north of the equator discovered the island they called Hawaii. They were ahead of the Englishman Capt. James Cook by more than 1,500 years. Cook "rediscovered" the islands in 1778, naming the volcanic group in honor of his financial benefactor, the Earl of Sandwich. The natives disagreed with some of Cook's ideas concerning private property and killed him in a brief encounter on the shore of Kealakekua Bay.

Standing on the south shore of Maui, looking across Alenuihaha Channel at the profile of Hawaii Island, with lava flows spotting the hillsides and palms fringing the shore edged by frothy surf, the viewer sees almost a replica of Savaii Island seen from Upolu in Western Samoa. The first Pacific explorers sailing from Samoa named Hawaii after their home. It was the image of their birthplace.

• • •

In the old days bananas were reserved for men. The penalty was death for the woman who ate one. Neither could the women eat with the men—they ate separately—afterwards. A careless commoner who allowed his shadow to fall across the path of a chief faced immediate death. The women and children of defeated warriors were killed without mercy.

For over 600 years, until the *kapu* (taboos) were deliberately violated and the old religion discarded, the benevolent ruling chiefs granted total amnesty to everyone who reached *pu'uhonua,* or place of refuge, in South Kona at Honaunau. The unfortunate refugee had only to enter the sacred area within the great encircling wall barricading the landside, or swim across Honaunau Bay to the *heiau* (temples). Inside was an inviolable haven for defeated warriors and breakers of a *kapu.* They were sanctified by a native priest and released under the protection of ruling chiefs and refuge gods—the spirits of dead chiefs.

The extraordinary wall, now protected in the City of Refuge National Historical Park, is more than 1,000 feet long, about 12 feet high and 17 feet thick, made of fitted stone, some many tons in size, handlaid without mortar. Twenty-two ruling chiefs were interred here, where they remained until 1829, when the giant carved idols and sacred bones were removed by Queen Regent Kaahumanu and hidden. They have never been found.

Kilauea is described as one of the world's most active volcanoes. Kilauea, perched on the slopes of Mauna Loa, but geologically independent, feeds separate volcanic vents through complex rift zones that crack the earth open southeast and southwest of Halemaumau, the main vent in Hawaii Volcanoes National Park.

The vent's collapsed pit crater gradually fills as repeated eruptions extrude magma into a lake of fire. Volcanic pressures are sometimes released by weak sections of the earth's crust many miles distant at Kapoho, where molten rock flows into the sea in a spectacular display of volcanism.

PAHOEHOE LAVA

The volcanic birth of Hawaii Island is clearly revealed where eruptions destroyed the Kilauea forest to build a new mountain, carved a rugged gorge at Akaka Falls with rain-spawned streams, and created Kaimu black sand beach from lava rock. The Devastation Trail in Hawaii Volcanoes National Park is a boardwalk laid by naturalists into the beginning of the earth to view the regeneration of growing plants stripped by a hot cinder shower. Black sand was produced in ancient littoral explosions when molten lava flowed into the resisting ocean at remote Kalapana.

153 VOLCANO ISLAND

NAHUE GULCH, HAMAKUA

'OHI'A-LEHUA

What is the use of a house if you haven't got a tolerable planet to put it on?
—Thoreau

ANTHURIUMS IN PUNA FOREST

Overleaf: HAMAKUA COAST ❧

Early Hawaiians conceived of a sacred place of refuge available to vanquished foes even in the midst of battle. The commoner who aroused the ire of ruling chiefs was able to seek sanctuary and forgiveness in the City of Refuge at Honaunau in Kona. Now, the world seeks refuge in Kona and Maui, and on Kauai, Molokai, and Oahu. Today's Hawaii is not a city of refuge—not a temple—perhaps not even a place of escape. Hawaii may be the promise of a new life.

May the visitor to Hawaii tread gently.
They are the only islands we have.

—R.W.

LILIUOKALANI PARK, HILO